Global Food Interdependence
Challenge to United States Policy

GLOBAL FOOD

INTERDEPENDENCE

Challenge to American Foreign Po

New York **Columbia University Press** *1980*

RAYMOND F. HOPKINS
&
DONALD J. PUCHALA

338.1
H 795 g

Library of Congress Cataloging in Publication Data

Hopkins, Raymond F
  Global food interdependence.

  Includes bibliographical references and index.
  1. Food supply.   2. Food supply—United States.
3. Economic assistance, American.   I. Puchala,
Donald James, 1939–   joint author.   II. Title.
HD9000.5.H66   338.1′9′73   80-11269
ISBN 0-231-04858-0
ISBN 0-231-04859-9 pbk.

Columbia University Press
New York   Guildford, Surrey

80-10042

To

Carol	*Jeanne*
Mark	*Susan*
Kathryn	*Elizabeth*
	Madeline

Contents

Figures

Tables

Preface

American eminence in food affairs is long and pervasive. The United States accounts for over half of the world's grain exports. It is important, therefore, to understand the role this vital resource plays in American diplomacy. Inescapably, choices made in the United States affect the prices, flow of trade, incentives for production, and degree of food security for other countries. A large number of policies determined by American political leaders affect total food production and consumption, including research priorities, import barriers, and land-use restrictions. Our study, however, emphasizes those policies that more directly and immediately affect international affairs, namely production, trade, and aid policies. Questions raised in these areas are the principal focus of diplomatic conversation and have the greatest impact upon American foreign relations.

The predominance of the United States, and North America, in shaping world food and agricultural matters has a long history. More important than gold and minerals among America's first exports were agricultural goods. Crops from the new world such as maize (corn), manioc and groundnuts (peanuts), introduced into Africa in the sixteenth century, spurred the settlement of the forested central part of the continent, allowing for large migration and population growth. Today they are the most important food crops of Subsaharan Africa. Cotton (admittedly not a food crop) was the prominent export in nineteenth century America; its earnings helped finance

American industrialization. By the twentieth century, the United States became the major supplier of foodstuff in the world; and the crop that dominated all others was wheat. The trend toward relying on American agriculture for food was first manifest in the emergency food relief provided by the United States, under Herbert Hoover after World War I. During World War II and immediately after, even prior to Marshall Plan aid, food aid from the United States played a large role in stabilizing Europe and alleviating malnutrition worldwide.

American diplomacy was at the heart of the forces leading to the founding of the Food and Agriculture Organization in 1946, now a specialized United Nations body. American food exports, especially wheat and to a lesser extent rice and feed grains, continue to grow. In the early 1960s, U.S. wheat exports accounted for over half of the world's trade and over half of those exports were on concessional or grant terms. (The Department of Agriculture was not only administering a major portion of U.S. foreign aid, but was also actively shaping trade policy and foreign production incentives.) A decade later, the reliability and generosity of American food policy were jeopardized by a changing world economic environment. Global production shortfalls, cutbacks in American production, growing domestic budget and inflationary pressures, and the steep increases in the cost of energy imports, led to a "crisis" in global food affairs and dramatic changes in American performance. In 1974 food aid fell from 50 percent to 5 percent of grain exports, while the trade balance in agriculture went from a small deficit to a 12 billion dollar surplus. American grain stocks, plus grain diverted from animal feeding, were exported to help stabilize supplies in Russia, Europe, and Japan, and to avert famine disasters in Africa and Asia—but nearly all on commercial terms. The vulnerability of less-developed countries to food shortages was dramatically revealed by famine conditions that developed in West Africa, Ethiopia, and Bangladesh, which directly contributed to violent changes of government.

This book grows out of the attention that these developments commanded among foreign-policy elites in 1974. In November of that year, Henry Kissinger, U.S. Secretary of State, opened a World Food Conference he had helped organize with the urging that "within a decade no child should go to bed hungry." As we complete this book in 1979, few of the twenty-odd resolutions of this conference have come to fruition. No international undertaking on food security or grain storage exists, food-aid flows remain at or below the minimum targets, and much of the urgency to address food problems has dissolved, leaving new institutions such as the World Food Council and the International Fund for Agricultural Development with mandates that exceed their practical authority and resources.

It is our purpose to clarify the role of American policy in the context of global food affairs. In doing this, we go beyond historical description and analysis to offer our own recommendations for renewed American leadership in addressing world food problems, whose capacity to again unsettle national governments and international intercourse remains dormant and mammoth. We urge that postures, strategies, and policies that we favor be examined critically by the reader. In the international politics of food there is, as with most things, no easy or clearly correct choice. To reduce the risk that food shortages or imbalances will again destabilize world affairs and bring personal suffering to the world's poorest peoples is not a costless exercise.

Just as this book was about to be printed, the United States took one of the most dramatic steps ever taken in food diplomacy. In response to the Soviet invasion of Afghanistan, in December 1979, President Carter declared an embargo on grain shipments to the USSR. Never in recent history has the withholding of food for noncommercial, political reasons been undertaken by the United States.

The idea of such politically motivated "food power" diplomacy was raised in the 1974–75 period, and in this book we have repeatedly argued against it as a tool of American policy. The action of withholding fourteen million tons of U.S. food (approximately 4 tons of wheat and 10 tons of corn) has had few immediate consequences. Increased domestic reserves are creating greater support for food aid, and prices and farm incomes are being supported by federal commitments to purchase embargoed wheat. Costs to taxpayers will be between two and three billion dollars. Events in 1980 and 1981, however, will yield the key evidence. Only then will we know whether the Soviets have been dissuaded politically or whether the basis for collaborative food trade between the U.S. and the USSR has been eroded. Even though the eight million tons of grain guaranteed by the United States to the Soviet Union in the 1975 trade agreement was not embargoed by Carter's decision, the Soviets may not be interested in future collaboration on food affairs. They may also find food elsewhere in the world, such as Brazil or Argentina, and thereby move away from food interdependence with the United States. We fear, therefore, that the use of food power in 1980 will prove as counter-productive as analysis contained in this book forecasts.

In preparing this manuscript we are indebted to a number of people. For intellectual stimulation and advice we especially thank Cheryl Christensen, Mac Destler, John Ferch, Joseph Gavin, Catherine Gwin, Dale Hathaway, Barbara Huddleston, Robert Keohane, Carol Lancaster, Ed Martin, Dan Morrow, Henry Nau, Roger Porter, Ed Schuh, Mitchell Wallerstein, and all the participants of the Conference on Global Food Interdependence held at Airlie House, Virginia, April 7–9, 1977. For assistance in typing the manuscript we are grateful to Sarah MacMillan. For financial support during various stages of our collaboration we must thank the Rockefeller Foundation, Columbia University, Swarthmore College, and most emphatically, the External Research Division of the Bureau of Intelligence and Research, Department of State, for whom an earlier version of the manuscript was prepared.

Raymond F. Hopkins and Donald J. Puchala   *January 1980*

Global Food Interdependence
Challenge to United States Policy

CHAPTER 1

Food Problems
and the Policy Agenda

Global food interdependence is growing. International transactions critical in the production, distribution, and consumption of food link the world's countries and peoples with ever stronger bonds. Since World War II, we have witnessed impressive changes in the world food system, including global integration of food and agricultural input markets, an enhanced international division of labor in agriculture, together with the decline of subsistence life styles, a spread of new technologies, and the introduction of food aid as an institutionalized feature of international relations. In all of this, the United States has played a leading role, fostering changes in the world food system, accelerating the pace of transformation, and nurturing new interdependence in both commodities and their management.

After centuries of recurrent famines and food shortages, food security during the 1950s and 1960s was realized to a large degree, thanks largely to the United States. This historically significant accomplishment of the United States was largely a by-product of domestic farm policies. These led directly to high production, government surpluses, and major U.S. efforts to create overseas markets; indirectly, they, in turn, assured the world of stable prices and ample supply.

Unfortunately, this era of food security has ended. Following 1972, the performance of the international food system and the reliability of the system's most important actor, the United States, have been seriously questioned. Problems in food interdependence became apparent, and ominous, under dramatic pressures of short-fall and shortage in the early 1970s—problems for which we have not yet found solutions. These global food problems critically affect human development and international relations. We begin our study of American policy by analyzing these problems; we conclude it by prescribing courses of action for the United States appropriate to solving them in the American and global interest.

Food problems, in the sense that we use the term, are *conditions* of production, distribution, or consumption that are sufficiently *undesirable* to at least some producers, distributors, or consumers that they are prompted to *initiate calls for change.*

Food problems rise and fall in relative importance depending upon who is worried about them and what effects they are expected to have. At one extreme, food problems have been portrayed as chaotic and growing dire. Revolutionary responses are advocated, including worldwide changes in land-tenure systems, trade policy, and government regulation.[1] At the opposite extreme, minor market improvements are suggested as ways to enhance the adjustment capacity of the current system.[2] A survey of what problems compete successfully for headline space in the *New York Times* shows a dramatic rise in attention given to food problems in 1973 and 1974, and a decline since then.[3] The flows of memos and agendas of meetings in the White House and State Department reportedly follow a similar trend during 1973–78.[4] What propelled food problems to the fore in the early 1970s was the lack of food security evidenced in shortages, cutbacks in food relief to poor countries, and sharply higher prices for American consumers.

Among food and agricultural experts, interest and attention have varied less dramatically. Needless to say, however, there is a lively debate among such experts over the long-term dimensions and severity of world food problems. The controversy stems from many sources, including differences in analysts' disciplinary training and ideological perspective, as well as from the varying data they call upon, the different forecasting and other methodological techniques they employ, and, not surprisingly, from crop and market conditions prevailing at the moment of analysis.[5] In general, our judgments on food policy are based on points of consensus among otherwise contending viewpoints, but as necessary we have not refrained from evaluating others' conclusions and framing our own arguments in the light of what seems the best evidence. Our recommendations tend to steer a middle course between the positions of those who minimize food problems and those who view problems as so severe as to require radical departures in policy. While undramatic, we believe they are nonetheless realistic and responsible.

Not one, but five problems are posed by existing world food conditions. First, we face the threat in the 1980s of *chronic food shortages* in some regions, most notably in South Asia and Africa, and with them economic, political, and human deprivations. Second, current arrangements in production and distribution allow *undesirable instability.* Initially, instability is in food supply, but this leads to unreasonable fluctuations in prices, unpredictable markets, and undependable trade flows. Third, and relatedly, certain poorer countries encounter the problem of *insecurity of food imports,* especially when imports represent important elements in national standards of living, and, more crucially, when they represent hedges against actual starvation. A fourth problem results from the *low productivity of agriculture* and related poverty in many less-developed countries. Such conditions represent a barrier to both food production and general economic development, as well as a costly waste of human resources. Fifth, there is *chronic malnutrition,* especially among underprivileged groups and classes in certain countries and regions.

Each of the five problems is significant and hence deserving of extended analysis. Yet the five global problems are obviously interrelated. Each is a cause of one or several of the others, and all lead to, or follow from, fundamental distortions of supply or demand for food. What makes the interrelatedness of global food problems analytically perplexing is that various elements of distributional distortion affect different countries and populations in different ways, sometimes at different times. As a result, the universality of the world food system, and the interdependence of its participants, tend to be blurred. Much of our argument and analysis is aimed at clarifying and addressing this interdependence and its implications. Throughout the chapters that follow, we emphasize: first, that no single or simple policy can solve all of the problems of the global food system; and second, that no course of action, American or otherwise, can succeed in the face of international resistance or even in the absence of international cooperation. By understanding complexities, practicable steps toward coordinating national and international action in mutually beneficial ways can be identified that will significantly alleviate the severity of world food problems.

Global Food Problems in Overview

Let us look more closely at each of the five problems as they occur on the agenda of world food diplomacy:

Food shortages in the early 1970s were responsible for the dramatic increases in the price of grain and other basic foodstuffs, and for heightened domestic and international political interest in food problems. The shortages that developed between 1972 and 1974 and their consequences were particularly severe due to the convergence of a rather unusual cluster of causal factors both in production and in government supply policy.[6] The continuing rise in world population, however, and the growing taste for meat are also important factors setting the stage for shortages.

Some analysts refer to the years 1973–74 as a period of "scarcity crisis" for the global food system. The term *crisis,* however, has emotional connotations and using it too frequently tends to destroy

its analytical relevance. Whether the term crisis is appropriate, therefore, is debatable; nevertheless 1973–74 were years of *extreme and
rapid change in global food supply and price conditions.* They were
dangerous years because food supplies were deteriorating toward the
point where prolonging the extraordinary conditions would have
resulted in major famines. The gravity of the situation as it developed
between 1972 and 1975 is captured rather dramatically in two sets of
indexes: (1) grain export prices; and (2) reserve stocks of grains as
reported in tables 1.1 and 1.2.

Note in the tables how prices begin their steep rise and total
reserves begin their deterioration in the summer of 1972. Although
some American idle land was put into production in 1973 to meet the
situation, prices continued to climb and total reserves dwindled.

Table 1.1 Average Wheat Export Prices, 1968–78
Dollars/bushel (60 lbs.); averaged for grades and varieties

Year	United States	Canada[a]	Australia[b]
1968	1.69	1.96	1.42
1969	1.67	1.89	1.38
1970	1.74	1.71	1.33
1971	1.69	1.70	1.40
1972	1.86	1.89	1.54
1973	3.55	4.37	2.77
1974	5.16	6.22	3.72
1975	4.79	5.52	3.11[c]
1976	3.64	4.01	2.96
1977[d]	2.86	3.35	–
1978	3.53	4.14	–

SOURCES: United Nations, *Monthly Bulletin of Statistics* (December 1976), 30 (12): 165, for
1968–75; and *Foreign Agricultural Trade of the United States:* (December 1977, p. 83, and
January 1979, pp. 64–65.

[a]Canadian dollars.
[b]Australian dollars.
[c]Figure is for June 1976.
[d]Figures for 1977 and 1978 are for U.S. number 2 hard winter and Canadian number 1.

Table 1.2   World Food Reserves, 1960/61 to 1977/78

	Reserve Stocks Of Grain[1]	Grain Equivalent of Idled U.S. Cropland	Total World Reserves	Reserves as Days of Annual Grain Consumption
		(million metric tons)		
1960/61	168	68	236	103
1961/62	180	81	261	112
1962/63	154	70	224	93
1963/64	157	70	227	94
1964/65	152	71	223	88
1965/66	155	78	233	88
1966/67	130	51	181	68
1967/68	157	61	218	79
1968/69	175	73	248	87
1969/70	208	71	279	93
1970/71	193	41	234	76
1971/72	155	78	233	73
1972/73	172	24	196	60
1973/74	127	0	127	37
1974/75	132	0	132	40
1975/76	123	0	123	37
1976/77	126	0	126	36
1977/78[2]	151	0	151	43

SOURCE: Worldwatch Institute, Washington, D.C.: compiled from data published by the U.S. Department of Agriculture. Reported in Martin McLaughlin, *The United States and World Development Agenda 1979* (New York: Praeger, 1979), p. 189.

[1]Based on carry-over stocks of grain at the beginning of the crop year in individual countries for year shown. Stock levels include reserve stocks of importing as well as of exporting countries.

[2]Preliminary estimate.

However, a key factor affecting the price at which grains moved internationally in this period is not the total working stocks in the world, but rather the stocks of exporting countries. Many large importing countries maintain working stocks that because of export barriers are seldom available for export, especially during periods of shortage, and hence are not directly a factor in international market prices. Rather it is the stocks of the exporting countries that both

Table 1.3 Wheat and Coarse Grains in World Trade
Exporting Country[a] Supply Situation
(in million metric tons)

Average	Exporting Countries Beginning Stock		Working[b] Stocks		Total Use: Export and Consumption		Beginning Stock as % of Total Use	
	Wheat	Coarse Grains	Wheat	Coarse Grains	Wheat	Coarse Grains	Wheat	Coarse Grains
60/61–70/71	42.7	60.7	10.4	24.4	68.3	180.7	64	36
71/72	44.4	40.4	12.6	38.4	75.5	224.6	59	18
72/73	41.4	55.4	12.8	30.3	88.3	244.3	47	23
73/74	22.7	37.0	15.0	33.0	82.3	247.4	28	15
74/75	19.8	29.3	14.0	33.4	80.5	209.5	25	14
75/76[c]	22.3	26.8	13.7	28.3	87.1	218.2	26	13
76/77	29.5	24.3	14.8	29.5	87.4	228.9	34	11
77/78	46.8	37.0	14.9	30.9	91.4	243.1	51	15
78/79	44.9	51.5	15.5	32.8	92.0	255.5	49	20

SOURCES: Philip H. Tresize, *Rebuilding Grain Reserves Toward an International System* (Washington, D.C.: Brookings Institution, 1976), pp.8–9 and Food and Agriculture Organization, *Food Outlook* (Rome: January 23, 1979) pp. 18–20.

[a]Exporting countries are United States, Canada, Australia, and Argentina for wheat, and include Thailand and S. Africa for coarse grains.

[b]Stocks in the "pipeline," that is, already committed to specific future uses and hence unavailable for alternative allocations. Using Tresize's estimates of 17% of the previous years' disappearance (consumption plus exports) for wheat and 13.5% for coarse grains (Tresize, p. 7, n. 5.).

[c]Coarse grain figures for 1976 are interpolated.

provide the security for deficit countries' food needs and prove the major variable affecting prices and control over markets. Comparing table 1.3 and table 1.1, one finds that the price of wheat mounted in 1973 and 1974 as wheat supplies tightened and most dramatically *as the stocks of exporters declined.* Coarse grain prices and stocks followed a similar pattern, although with less precipitous price changes, but with a greater drop in consumption within exporting countries.

World prices became most extreme in 1974 (the first half of 1974 to be exact) when they peaked at postwar highs, nearly four times above 1968 levels. World reserves fell to a two-decade low, to the point where the world held only thirty-three days' consumption of grain in storage (and some countries held much less!). Although stock-scarcity conditions among exporters continued to be strained into 1975 and 1976, production gains in importing countries, especially in Southeast Asia, and declining consumption, especially in the United States, reduced market pressures and allowed prices to drop. As of 1976, world reserves (table 1.2) were still critically low. There had been no replacement of exporters' reserves and the import-dependent world was still eating largely from month to month. During 1977 and 1978, with production at or above trend, surpluses began to build, especially among exporters. (See table 1.3.). There has, however, been but slight gain in per capita food available globally, and whether current surpluses provide real protection against a global shortage in the future is doubtful. In lowest-income countries, per capita calories declined overall from 1973 to 1977 by 5.5 percent.[7]

The years 1972–75, then, are benchmarks in the analysis of global food problems. By hindsight, their greatest significance lies in the fact that they prompted a long overdue and sober analysis of the global food system. It must be borne in mind, however, that regardless of the apparent uniqueness of contributing factors, shortages in 1973 and 1974 fundamentally reflected the global growth in demand for food stimulated by rapidly expanding population in many less-developed countries, and by shifts toward higher protein diets in more affluent countries. In this sense, scarcities in trade markets in 1973 and 1974 were extraordinary only as regards their unprecedented severity, and improvements in supply conditions since 1975 by no means suggest that food scarcity is on the way to being fundamentally overcome, either in world trade, or most especially in poor countries. While stocks of exporters offered a greater margin of security in 1978 than in 1973–74, they have not returned to the levels of security prevailing in the 1960s. For example, in the sixties, exporter wheat stocks, exclusive of working stocks (see table 1.3), were 80 percent of exports, and coarse grain stocks were 136 percent. These stocks dropped in 1973 and 1974 to 16 percent and 12 percent of wheat exports and 7 percent and 8 percent of coarse grains. By 1978, stocks climbed, but only to 51 percent and 25 percent respectively, no more than half the relative position of the 1960s.

Despite uncertainties in export supplies over the next decade, and taking into account some analysts' pessimism, many who have looked into production problems in agriculture can identify adequate resources in the years ahead, which, if utilized, could meet growing demands, including demands based on a desire for better diets. Yet, this capacity is in question because of the uncertainty that less-developed countries will increase their domestic production. This increase will only be realized if potential research and technology gains are acted upon, if requisite investments are made, and if all other varieties of output-enhancing opportunity are grasped. For several less-developed countries, this means stemming declining rates of domestic per capita food production. For others, it means pushing agricultural growth rates toward four or five or six percent a year.

Instability marked by extreme and erratic fluctuations in commodity prices has come to characterize and confuse international agricultural markets in recent years. Global supplies of foodstuffs and their prices have fluctuated markedly and erratically from year to year since 1972, compared to the earlier two decades. This is due mainly to changing weather conditions, and in some measure also to variations in farmers' planting strategies and in government-promoted incentives and disincentives. But until the 1970s, major fluctuations in production have prompted only minor changes in price due to the fact that during most of the post–World War II era the United States and Canada accumulated large reserves in periods of surplus and were able to release them in periods of shortage thus buffering price shifts. But such large public reserves no longer exist, and North American policies no longer encourage their accumulation. The farmer-held reserves that have accumulated in the United States since 1977 are neither as available nor as large as stocks held by the government (CCC) in the 1960s. Therefore, unless policies and capacities change, we have a situation wherein even mild shifts (less than 2 percent) in world supply can, and do, bring about abrupt and extreme fluctuations in price.

Price instability tends to skew rewards from market participation toward those who can best afford to speculate or to otherwise endure shifting extremes. Conversely, it imposes penalties from market dependence upon those who can least easily and least quickly adjust to fluctuation—namely lower-income countries, in general, and lower-income consumers, in particular. Beyond adjustment effects, fluctuating world food prices also tend to wreak havoc with public and private economic planning, again, most notably in less-developed countries where planners must estimate food costs in their national development plans. In addition, in developed food-exporting countries, large market fluctuations stimulate political discontent among farmers, as is frequently the case in the United States and in several Common Market countries. The American Farm Movement, for instance, disrupted Washington for over a month in January-March, 1979, with a "tractor-cade." While it is certainly the case that some price instability may be beneficial for calling forth appropriate market adjustments, evidence from recent experience suggests that price fluctuations outside of a rather restricted range rapidly become dysfunctional.

Securing food imports in many poor countries has become a recurring problem of considerable magnitude. Food is transferred internationally via two channels: trade and aid. Simply stated, the problem facing any number of less-developed countries is that both of these channels have intermittently become less reliable sources of supply. Price inflation in foodstuffs and competing demand from industrialized countries such as Japan and the Soviet Union limit LDC access to the international commercial system. Industrial countries' willingness to extend aid, which has tended to fluctuate more according to domestic and international political expediencies than to needs for food, similarly constrains LDC access to the international concessional system. What periodically changes this import problem into a supply crisis is that many of the most populous less-developed countries, notably India and Bangladesh, possess extremely limited capacities to adjust to internal shortfalls by reducing the use of cereals for animal feeding so that imports intermittently become the difference between meager diets and starvation. As figure 1.1 illustrates, in 1974–76, India, Bangladesh and other developing countries spent millions of dollars on agricultural exports from the United States—exports that, unlike earlier years, came heavily on commercial rather than subsidized terms. Relying on increasing imports, however, cannot be the solution to the scarcity problems of the food-deficit LDCs. Poor countries and peoples will lose out if they must compete for scarce international supplies with the rich. Yet, even the most optimistic projections of exporters' production show future shortfalls, compared to projected needs, of as much as 180 million tons for LDCs by 1990 (see figure 1.4).[8] Still some guarantees of internationally supplied food on concessional terms must be affirmed for decades ahead. Otherwise supply crises will cloud and confuse rational efforts toward internal development.

With regard to the dependence of developed countries upon external food supplies, the issue of insecurity is bound more closely to concerns for macroeconomic stability than to fears of starvation. For countries such as Japan, the Soviet Union, certain Common Market

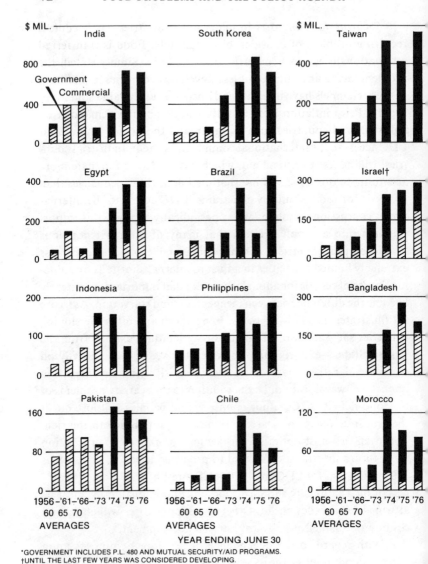

*GOVERNMENT INCLUDES P.L. 480 AND MUTUAL SECURITY/AID PROGRAMS.
†UNTIL THE LAST FEW YEARS WAS CONSIDERED DEVELOPING.

SOURCE: FATUS (Washington, D.C.: U.S. Dept. of Agriculture, July 1977), p.16.

Figure 1.1
**U.S. Agricultural Exports to Developing Countries Government and
Commercial, Fiscal Years***

members, and newly industrializing states like South Korea, predictable access to global markets, and reasonable prices on these markets, facilitate the execution of national economic policies, and the efficient allocation of domestic resources. Threats to external food supplies therefore become threats to economic stability and growth and detriments to the political-economic foundations of modern welfare states. Recent experience has shown the Japanese to be especially sensitive to the threat that imports may be cut off; since the Japanese have declined from 80 percent self-sufficiency in food in 1960 to relying on imports for about half their food supply (as measured by original calories), the prospect of a supply cutoff from the U.S., which provides over one-fourth of her agricultural imports, can inject sizable tensions into Japanese-American diplomacy.[9] Nevertheless, the major increase in U.S. food exports in recent years has been to less-developed, not developed countries (see figure 1.2). The overall world-grain-import picture shows that the European Economic Community (EEC) and Japanese exports grew only .6 million tons

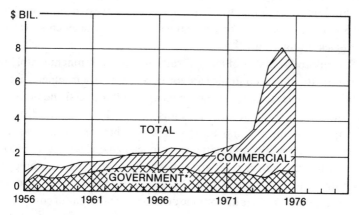

*Includes Public Law 480 and Mutual Security Programs.
SOURCE: FATUS (Washington, D.C.: U.S. Department of Agriculture, July 1977), p. 17.

Figure 1.2
U.S. Agricultural Exports to Developing Countries

from 1976 to 1978 (all due to Japanese increases in coarse grain imports) while imports of East Asian, African, Near Eastern, and Latin American countries grew from 51 to 67.7 million tons, a growth of 33 percent in two years.[10]

Low productivity and poverty plague millions of the world's populace engaged in agriculture. The rural populations of the less-developed countries, constituting 60 percent to 90 percent of these nations' peoples, account for more than half of the world's population. As a rural labor force they are a key potential resource for greater food production. In addition, of course, these poor people are in most need of more and better food. Their low productivity is at the heart of the supply side of the world food problem.[11]

In the most general way, it could be said that low productivities in peasant agriculture in Asia, Africa, and Latin America follow basically from the underemployment of land and labor. Technologies that would heighten the productivities of these factors are often not available. But, more fundamentally, what are lacking are educational facilities that would prepare farmers to employ more productive technologies, funds that would permit them to invest in more productive technologies, and markets that would offer inducements to technological innovations.[12]

Still, to look at problems of rural underdevelopment simply in terms of standard economic categories is to treat them superficially. Major obstacles to rural development are as often social and political as they are economic and technological.[13] Powerful traditional groups often oppose innovation and reform because such measures threaten their status and influence; modernizing elites prefer urban industrialization over rural investment; credit institutions, domestic and international, balk at small-size, hard-to-collect farm funding; international suppliers discourage development for fear of competing sales. And we could go on to cite even more unsavory obstacles to rural development, such as programmatic racism and ethnic repression.[14]

Forces are currently pushing for rural modernization and increased productivity in LDCs, and on balance the situation is not totally discouraging.[15] Still, given the monumental efforts compelled by increasing demand, the time involved in enhancing human resources, and the limited means available, progress toward heightened peasant productivity is likely to be slow and halting in the years ahead—too slow, and too halting, perhaps, to meet the supply crises projected for the 1980s.[16]

Malnutrition is both the most general and the most basic world food problem. By shifting attention from production and aggregate distribution problems to the actual consumption of food, the most intractable elements of world food problems are revealed.[17] Malnutrition, estimated variously to afflict at least one-half to perhaps over one billion people, is substantially a product of poverty; most people suffer from dietary deficiencies because they or their families cannot afford more or better food. The inequality of income that determines undernourishment is an international problem, and resultant malnutrition deserves special attention not only because it is so widespread, but because it requires different targets and different institutions to remedy it than does a food problem defined merely as low productivity.

The problems of malnutrition and starvation relate directly to inequalities of income globally and within countries. In Asian and African countries, the bulk of the populations consume far less than the recommended daily caloric intake of 2,450 calories. A country like Brazil had an average per capita caloric intake of 2,541 in 1964–66, but about 44 percent of its population was malnourished.[18]

Guaranteeing the poor a decent chance to enjoy basic human satisfactions requires attention to their well-being—for well-being, rather than wealth, is the fundamental value of which they are deprived. While those in poor countries are unlikely to gain great improvements in material wealth in the coming decades, they can readily have improvements in their basic well-being. Farmers and urban workers need not continue to suffer the draining effects of malnutrition or chronic underemployment (which, itself, reflects the weakened health and low energy levels of undernourished persons). Some poor countries have been able to overcome these problems to a degree. As noted in chapter 6, China and India pose contrasting examples; and Sri Lanka, which has about the same level of GNP per capita as India, has achieved a nutritionally better quality of life than either India or China.

Solutions to problems of malnutrition are costly and complex. They involve dealing with health conditions in slums, facilities in rural areas, and cultural patterns which are often counternutritional. A broad attack on malnutrition would have to involve, at a minimum, better mechanisms for distributing food, as well as efforts to increase economic growth. Simple calculations of the amount of additional calories needed by those now malnourished to close the "nutrition gap" suggest that an additional 25 million tons of grain would suffice and would provide an additional 500 calories for the half-billion malnourished in the poorest countries. But this solution assumes that such additional amounts of grain would in fact be made available as transfers from grain-producing countries to grain-importing countries and that the grain would be distributed equitably to the malnourished in these countries. No one is even proposing this. Furthermore, any international distribution system would require great intrusion into the domain of national sovereignty, since neither market nor administrative means for such distribution now exist. The other option, however, relying on additional economic growth and market adjustments to result automatically in higher food consumption for the poor will certainly fail. An across-the-board rise in income resulting in additional consumption would drive up prices, increase demand for grain feed for livestock, and have only a marginal effect on diets.[19] In short, market solutions will not solve malnutrition at any foreseeable time, and even if successful steps are taken to increase the aggregate amount of food available in the world and in each food-deficit country, chronic malnutrition with its long-run debilitation of human capacities, may continue largely unabated unless it is identified and approached as a separate and distinct food problem.

Factors Conditioning
Future Food Supply and Demand

What is the prospect that the five food problems raised here can be solved? This is difficult to assess, inasmuch as solutions will depend critically on what priorities and policies are adopted by various governments, international bodies, agribusinesses, and farmer/peasant organizations. It will depend, too, in substantial measure upon how Americans and the United States Government choose to respond to future challenges and opportunities in agriculture, trade, and aid. Such responses are the primary focus of this book. However, there are also physical, technological, and parametric social factors which will affect future outcomes in the global food system because they constrain effective choices of the world's peoples. In moving toward the analysis of food policies, therefore, it is important to understand some of these basic inert and inertial forces, for they both shape the problems we have just outlined and set the corridor within which solutions must be sought.

Factors Affecting Food Consumption

Numerous factors affect the food supply/demand equation. The production or supply side is the most difficult to forecast, both on a year-to-year basis and over the longer term. Demand, or consumption, on the other hand, is easier to forecast, at least under conditions of relatively stable prices, because its growth reflects the results of relatively slow, predictable, and in some cases seemingly inexorable processes of change. These differences are illustrated in the production and consumption patterns for grains, the major traded food commodities (see figure 1.3a, b). The relatively smooth growth pattern in consumption deviates from the trend line seriously only during the period of sharp instability in world markets in 1974–75 when dramatically high prices had their effect. The United States played a major role, in fact, in limiting this downturn in consumption as illustrated in the overall pattern of stockholding. The drawdown to offset declining production after 1972 was principally borne by the United States, as can be seen in figure 1.3c.

The growth of consumption is driven by essentially three factors: population expansion, shifts in taste, and growing discontent with malnutrition. Although population-growth forecasts have recently lowered expected world population for the year 2000 to nearer six billion than seven billion, this still represents a 50 percent increase over 1975–80 population levels. To sustain the life of youngsters

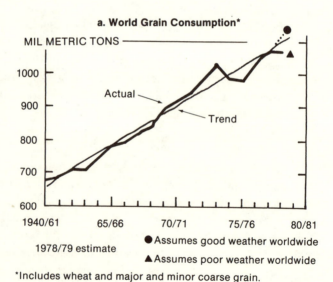

Figure 1.3
World Production, Consumption, and Carryover of Grain

b. World Grain Production*

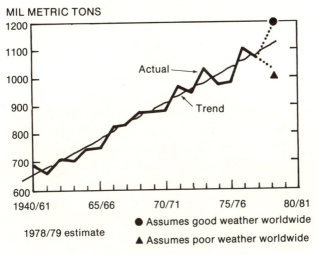

1978/79 estimate

● Assumes good weather worldwide
▲ Assumes poor weather worldwide

*Includes wheat and major and minor coarse grain.

c. World Carryover Stocks of Wheat and Coarse Grain

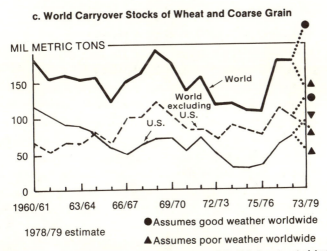

1978/79 estimate

●Assumes good weather worldwide
▲Assumes poor weather worldwide

SOURCE: *World Agricultural Situation,* no. 16 (Washington, D.C.: U.S. Department of Agriculture, Economics, Statistics, and Cooperative Service. July 1978), pp. 9–10.

Figure 1.3 (Continued)

already born and growing toward adult consumption levels—as well as to feed the additional population born in the next 20 years—simply at current consumption levels, will require a substantial increase in food production. Since population increases are forecast to occur most heavily in regions currently nutritionally deficient, if all increased production were channeled to localities in direct proportion to their population increases, existing levels of consumption could be maintained with substantially less increase in aggregate production than the percentage of population growth; this is because the high growth areas consume less than the world average now. However, markets do not operate to distribute food in this fashion, as we already know.[20]

Rising affluence, both among elites in the poorer countries of the world and in the middle classes of the increasingly prosperous countries such as Japan, Brazil, Nigeria, and Iran, suggest that "effective" demands for meat and other products that require greater resources in the form of feed grains, grazing land, and labor for production, processing, and storage, will outstrip population growth and lead to a substantial increase in total world demand, a demand increase quite differently distributed than the increase in population.

Finally, though more speculative, is the prospect that growing attention focused on the economic, social, and political costs of undernutrition will expand demand. For instance, poor-country elites and representatives of undernourished portions of populations in countries whose average caloric intake seems satisfactory, such as Brazil, are likely to implement policies to expand nutrition and food welfare programs. Subsidizing food to enhance the diets of the poor in a country's populace is increasingly common, with examples ranging from the food-stamp program of the United States to the fair-price shop system in India.[21] Various projections about future consumption have been made. For example, the Food and Agriculture Organization (FAO) projects increases in grain consumption in the twenty years, 1970 to 1990, of approximately 230 million metric tons in industrialized countries, 385 million tons in "developing market economies," and 120 million tons in "developing centrally planned economies"—a total world increase of about 60 percent.[22] Considerable skepticism about projections, however—particularly those beyond ten to fifteen years—is warranted. Evaluations of predictions of various kinds indicate that their reliability decreases dramatically after a few years and that forecasting the future is of little utility beyond 15 years.[23] For example, in 1970, the Department of Agriculture predicted production, consumption, and trade in grain for 1980. Table 1.4 compares the results of the most optimistic option—high production, low prices, and high trade with the actual 1978 results. Note that U.S. production in 1978 was 26 million tons lower than the 1980 prediction, but exports were 29 million tons above it!

This third factor of consumption growth, discontent with malnutrition, results from the increasing attention given to nutritional deficiencies and the negative health and economic consequences that flow from these. This increased attention is reflected in the expanded programs of the FAO and the United States Agency for International Development (AID) to promote nutrition planning in less-developed countries and to expand food aid programs that are nutritionally targeted. The White House study on food and hunger completed in 1978 led to a Presidential Commission whose title included both "Hunger and *Malnutrition.*" The International Food Policy Research Institute (IFPRI), an authoritative independent research group, has begun making two sets of estimates, one based on projected market demand and the other based on additional demand if dietary requirements are to be met. It seems significant that they are beginning to estimate future production goals in terms of meeting nutritional needs. Furthermore, work is expanding on nutritional concerns as evidenced in growing budgets and staffs at national institutes of health and in the expanded activity of the MIT-Harvard Nutrition Policy Program, which has begun programs with the

**Table 1.4 Predicted and Actual Grain Production,
Consumption, and Trade**
(in million metric tons)

		Predicted Maximum: 1980[a]	Actual: 1978[b]
World	Production	1,416	1,408
	Consumption	1,401	1,367
U.S.	Production	291	265
	Consumption	226	167
	Trade	57	86
Developed Countries (excluding Canada, Australia and New Zealand)	Production	157	174
	Consumption	225	205
	Trade	−56	−33
LDCs (excluding Argentina)	Production	378	367
	Consumption	420	427
	Trade	−40	−52
Socialist (USSR, China, Eastern Europe)	Production	439	515
	Consumption	445	539
	Trade	−6	−36

SOURCE: [a]*World Demand Prospects for Grain in 1980,* (Washington D.C.: U.S. Dept. of Agriculture, 1971), pp. 72–75;
[b]*Foreign Agriculture Circular on Grains,* (Washington D.C.: U.S. Dept. of Agriculture, December 1978), p. 38.

NOTE: Grain includes wheat, rice, and coarse grains.

United Nations University. All these actions foreshadow or, perhaps, reflect a continuing trend of giving greater attention to human health and to the nutritional basis of it.

Let us consider projections of future world demand. As done by IFPRI, they take into account the three most estimatable factors: median-population-growth estimates, the effect of various rates of economic development on effective demand and dietary habits, and the increased demand for adequate nutrition. These projections forecast substantial and regular increases in effective demand. For example, as shown in figure 1.4, the International Food Policy Research

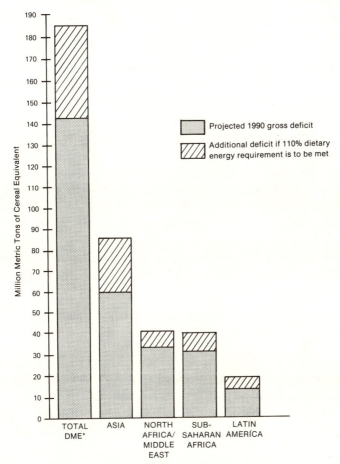

SOURCE: International Food Policy Research Institute *Food Needs of Developing Countries* (Washington, D.C.: IFPRI, 1977), p. 53.

Figure 1.4
Projected 1990 Gross Deficits to Meet Market Demand and Energy Standards in Developing Market Economies, by Region

Institute projects a gross deficit under current trends of 185 million metric tons of grain to meet the energy requirements of populations in developing countries (and this excludes "Socialist" countries such as China and North Korea).[24] When surpluses from the few exporting countries among this poor-country group are added to the projected surpluses of grain that exporting developed countries are likely to supply, the IFPRI estimate is that a shortfall would be between 84 and 107 million metric tons. There are, of course, a number of other factors that go into the disappearance of food supplies other than direct human consumption. These include losses incurred in harvesting; loss to mildew and rot in grain storage and transport; waste in food-processing industries; and finally, losses in individual household consumption, most predominantly reflected in the edible foodstuffs delivered to the sewage and waste disposal systems in the United States.[25] (Further food is "lost" when grain is fed to animals that, while subsequently consumed, provide far less food value than the orginal calories in the grain.)

Factors Affecting Food Production

The factors affecting production or supply of foodstuffs are more diverse and less predictable than those affecting "disappearance" or consumption. Land is the most important resource input for food production. The fertility of land can change slowly as ecological factors enrich soils through organic decomposition or deplete soils through erosion, leaching, salinization, and other productivity-destroying changes both natural and socially induced.[26] The availability of fertile land has declined markedly in the twentieth century as it has been removed from production by urbanization and industrialization. Urban growth and highways alone remove hundreds of thousands of acres from production each year, not only in the United States farm belt, but in fertile areas around growing Asian cities such as Shanghai and Bangkok. Furthermore, access to land is itself not a freely exchangeable good, responsive to market conditions. Rather it is one of the fundamental bases of various political systems. Property rights and land tenure represent the major factor affecting the distribution of privilege among world societies.[27] Because of such conditioning factors, the availability of additional land to expand agricultural production is a subject of considerable uncertainty. The FAO background study for the 1974 World Food Conference suggested that considerable land suitable for agriculture could be brought under cultivation if additional demand warranted it (that is, made it economically attractive.)[28] A study by the Economic and Social Institute of the Free University at Amsterdam is even more optimistic; it estimated that, as of 1965, only 39 percent of potentially suitable agricultural land was being used and only 3.2 percent of maximum agricultural productivity was being realized. Of the various regions of the world, Japan was seen as the closest to realizing maximum production from its land, and Europe was closest to realizing full land utilization with 88 percent of its arable land under cultivation. (See table 1.5.)[29]

Optimistic estimates of the availability of additional land for expanding agricultural production, and other resources to increase land fertility, such as water, fertilizers, pesticides, improved seed and horticultural practices, overlook substantial barriers that exist to using them. To begin with, there are political and social constraints to bringing additional land under cultivation (such as wealthy and politically influential property owners who prefer that land be empty to increase their privacy, or to use the land for animal pasture). Furthermore, there are substantial problems in improving water and irrigation systems, such as improper drainage and salinization. There are also ecological barriers to consider in the use of increased chemical fertilizers and pesticides, and there are energy constraints on the production of chemicals used in their production, because many of them have a petroleum base and most require substantial energy in their production and transportation. Above all there are considerable problems in altering the techniques and practices of farmers, although whether these are a part of peasant culture or a reflection of

Table 1.5   Actual and Potentially Suitable Agricultural Land; Actual and Maximum Agricultural Production

	Arable Land in "1965" Mill. Ha (1)	Potentially Suitable Agric. Land Mill. Ha (2)	(1) in % of (2) (3)	Agric. Prod. in "1965" 10^8 Kg Cons. Prot. (4)	Maximum Agric. Prod. 10^8 Kg Cons. Prot. (5)	(4) in % of (5) (6)
Regions						
North America	220	546	40	397	7,159	5.6
Western Europe	129	147	88	233	2,192	10.7
Japan	6	8	72	29	111	25.9
Australia, etc.	59	284	21	86	3,723	2.3
Eastern Europe (Incl. USSR)	288	522	55	322	6,042	5.3
Subtotal Industrial economies	702	1,507	47	1,067	19,228	5.5
Latin America	122	695	18	173	14,599	1.2
Middle East	52	111	47	35	1,038	3.4
Tropical Africa	174	643	27	91	11,681	0.8
Southern Asia	266	382	70	248	7,520	3.3
China c.s.	111	349	32	267	3,992	6.7
Subtotal Developing Countries	725	2,180	33	815	38,830	2.1
World	1,427	3,687	39	1,882	58,058	3.2

SOURCE: Calculations mainly based on Food and Agriculture Organization data.

NOTE: "1965" refers to the average over the years 1964–66.

negative economic incentives is debatable.[30] In addition to the ecological, economic, and social constraints, there is still a basic question of whether the actual land area available for expansion is really as substantial as estimated. As suggested earlier, much of this land may be marginally productive and/or costly to bring into production in either political or economic terms. For instance, when the United States sought to achieve full production after 1973, a sizable portion of land that farmers had been paid to keep out of production was not returned. These "disappearing acres," which turned out to be marginal, or actually committed to other uses, are a good illustration of the problem. The world's most populous country, China, is especially land "tight" and limited in her capacity to expand production, and hence is a potentially large source of demand on world markets; this is inferrable from such simple but dramatic testimony that the space between the runways at Peking airport is sown with rice.[31] While we have evidence of dramatic increases in yield as a result of new miracle seeds combined with concerted government programs to support agricultural efforts, such as improved irrigation systems, easier access to credit, and extension services to advise farmers—as exemplified in the Punjab area of India—the extent to which this experience can be generalized is at best unknown. In any event, it demands a substantial mobilization of resources and commitment on the part of national and international political leaders.[32]

The list of constraints on higher production include, then, the uncertainty of how much land is really available (and how much land is currently being lost), the extent to which research breakthroughs may allow for higher yields (with "pessimism" to "uncertainty" characterizing scientific opinion),[33] the difficulty in developing the capital for financing agricultural development (for machinery, seeds, irrigation, fertilizer, pesticides, and so on), and the willingness of governments to develop the educational and extension services for rural areas, given the prevailing urban bias in most less-developed countries.[34] These constraints limit the prospects of growth or the quick application of research breakthroughs.

The most important variable affecting year-to-year variations in production is weather. Although trend is the best predictor of supply from one year to the next, weather variations are the major explanation of deviations from trend.[35] A recent study of weather and climate indicated extraordinary uncertainty among specialists as to the likely changes in weather patterns and overall climate in the next twenty years. On the whole, however, experts did look to increased year-to-year variability in weather compared to the "favorable" stability of the last two decades. This recent stability in the 1960s is shown in figure 1.5, which reports results of a model looking solely at the effects of climate in the U.S.—a large region. In general, declining weather stability will have a negative impact on overall production. The study's final results regarding the effect of weather on future prices, reserve requirements, and trade were not yet available, but the initial report suggests, by the broad uncertainties it reports and the considerable range for climatic change thought possible, that there is a risk of unknown size (but potentially substantial).[36] A serious weather-induced food shortfall would have a dramatic impact on production, with trade barriers, prices, inflation, and undernutrition all climbing steeply as a result. The central point of this review is that a risk of unknown proportion but one that implies substantial damage does exist.

Having acknowledged the multitude of factors affecting the production and consumption of world foodstuffs, and the vagaries of opinions among the experts as to how these complex factors are likely to mesh in the next decade or two, the problem we wish to focus on is how American and world policies have responded up to now to these conditions of uncertainty through various trading patterns, and through national and international management.

The Analysis of Food Policy

Chapters 2 through 5 of this volume are devoted to analyzing recent attempts to deal with the world food problems enumerated in this introduction. The emphasis in our analysis is upon the United

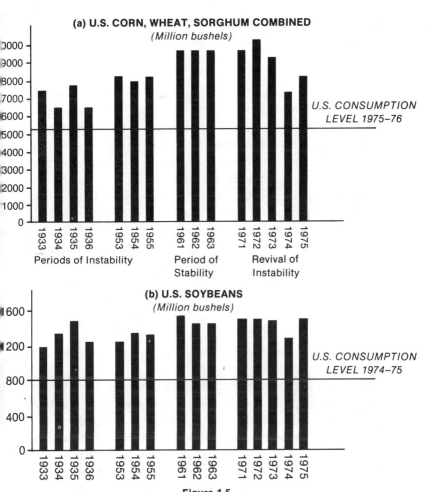

Figure 1.5
Expected Crop Fluctuations Due to Solely Climatic Variation, 1933–75

SOURCE: Kettering Foundation, *Impact of Climatic Fluctuation on Major North American Food Crops* (Columbus, Ohio 1975), p. 9.

States, and upon the goals, formulation, execution, and impacts of American foreign agricultural policy. Our central thesis is that the global food system has not been performing satisfactorily to solve outstanding problems in recent years. Hence, much of our evaluation is critical, and a number of our recommendations call for redirection in American efforts. Our criticisms, however, are not condemnations. We do not fix the blame for the world's ills upon the United States and its policies, and we do not realistically expect that even the wisest of American courses of action can bring positive results if unsupported by the international community.[37]

Chapter 2 is a review and analysis of United States participation in world food trade. The implications of American cereal-export dominance are explored, and the evolution of the international market is projected into the short-run future. Issues of trade liberalization and price stabilization are examined; American goals and interests are underlined; the course of our policy is mapped; and recommendations are made for future action. The thrust of these is that public policies are urgently needed to regulate vagaries, rectify distortions, and restrict abuses of the international market.

Chapter 3 takes up questions and issues concerning food aid. American interests in channeling concessional flows of foodstuffs are enumerated and elaborated. Linkages between food-aid policies and overall domestic and foreign agricultural policy are explored. Issues and options concerning the magnitude, direction, and duration of food aid are examined, and recommendations regarding future uses of food aid are made. Primary among the themes of chapter 3 are: first, a call for clarifying the priorities in United States food aid; second, an urging for the more direct tying of food aid to Third World development objectives; and third, a stress on the need for better evaluation of concessional food programs. All of these build from the basic proposition that food aid is useful to poor countries and is in the American interest to give, and that it should increase in the near future and probably continue in some forms indefinitely.

Chapter 4 is devoted to examining processes involved in the

making of United States foreign agricultural policy. At issue are questions concerning the balancing of interests and priorities among domestic and foreign policy constituencies and their spokesman, appropriate organization for food policy-making, appropriate assignments of leadership responsibility, and executive-congressional relations. Related matters have to do with expertise required in food policy-making, appropriate departmental assignments for food and agricultural specialists, and incentives to career development for specialists within government service. Among recommendations that follow from our analyses are: first, a call for more orderly interagency coordination; second, an urging for the greater appreciation of international food questions among senior officials; third, more delegation of responsibility to middle-level personnel; fourth, more positive congressional oversight; and fifth, better integration of private-sector and other nongovernmental actors into research, information gathering, and policy deliberations.

United States participation in international organizations dealing with world food problems is the subject of chapter 5. Here the history of early United States leadership in the FAO and other UN food, agriculture, and development agencies is reviewed and evaluated. Complexities and problems of multilateral cooperation are explored, and the accomplishments of food organizations are critically examined. The recent decline in American support for international food organizations, and this country's apparent retreat from leadership are noted with concern. Foremost among the recommendations of chapter 5 is the call for more active, more positive United States participation in world food organizations, more generous support and more imaginative leadership in the management of interdependence. Little in the analysis, however, implies that it is in the American interest, or in the global interest, that we should condone others' irresponsible behavior in world forums, that we should support unpromising (and unevaluated) programs, or that we should acquiesce in meaningless and wasteful institutional proliferation.

Chapter 6 shifts the focus of our analysis from the near term to the longer-run future. Two premises underlie this chapter's analyses. First, projecting global food and agricultural conditions into the future uncovers risks associated with widely varying global-supply situations. The uncertainty of projections follows from the exceedingly complex mix of factors that will combine to produce the future. It follows that uncertainty compounds as we move farther from the present. Yet, second, despite uncertainties, present policy and planning must embody anticipations of future developments, especially if adverse and undesirable outcomes are to be avoided. Day-to-day or week-to-week planning and action will not succeed where adjustment to avoid calamity requires decade-long programs. Consequently, chapter 6 reviews possible alternative developments in global food supply and demand for the period extending roughly to the end of this century. It also explores more and less probable causes for different developments, and it recommends appropriate policy responses to them in light of American goals. The overriding recommendation which follows from this analysis is that systematic consideration of probable futures should be directly and constantly integrated into present-day policy formulation.

Chapter 7 summarizes and systematizes the policy recommendations generated in preceding chapters. It embodies calls for continuity in areas where we have concluded that American policy is appropriately directed, and it stresses needs for change in areas where policy has displayed shortcomings. Five policy recommendations are accorded highest priority:

1. Greater stability in international food marketing should be guaranteed through policies directed toward instituting orderly marketing arrangements and a system of grain reserves.

2. Rural modernization in poor countries should be promoted with increased vigor.

3. The United States governmental organization for coordinating domestic and international food policy should be further integrated and revised to allow for more effective delegation of policy-implementing decisions.

4. Multilateral agencies should be accorded more support and use.

5. Important new programs of agronomic, economic, social, and political research should be initiated now to pave the way for more enlightened global food policies in years ahead.

Finally, a note on timeliness is in order. There is no question that food is more plentiful globally in 1979 than it was during and immediately after the "crisis" years of 1972–74, and it is therefore understandable why urgency has receded concerning food problems. Executive-branch officials have naturally turned from yesterday's crisis to today's, elected representatives have championed new causes and initiated new inquiries, and the mass media are exciting and educating their audiences with new concerns. With food problems, it appears that the creativity and dynamism spawned of crisis are ebbing rapidly, and many of the bold departures in commitment and organization taken at Rome in 1974 have lapsed or are bogging down in inertia. Yet it is more than likely that extraordinary food shortages will occur again long before the next decade has run its course, and it is disappointingly the case that neither the United States nor the world is presently any better prepared to deal with these than with earlier ones. Moreover, in many ways—social, political, economic, and moral—the *normal* state of the global food system continues to be unsatisfactory. Therefore, we encourage those who are reading this study to surmount today's relaxed policy atmosphere and to accept our recommendations in the same spirit of urgency and concern with which we propose them. There is nothing reassuring in the fact that we came through 1972–74 by the skin of our teeth. We simply cannot wait for the next crisis to mobilize us again, for by that time it will likely be too late to avoid extraordinary costs.

CHAPTER 2

The Commercial System: The Political Economy of Food Trade

Competition for advantage in food markets is no light matter. Within and among nations, control over markets and the flow of resources into and out of agriculture have been central matters for political dispute and protection of interests.[1] Tension and hostility derived from food-trade competition can affect national proclivities toward war and peace, as for example, the bitter rivalry between landed elites competing to sell Prussian rye and Russian wheat that helped propel European politics toward World War I.[2]

In the contemporary world, competition for food markets has receded as a political problem; the dominant features serving to ameliorate or exacerbate the global food problems outlined in Chapter 1 are allocations and prices in commercial food trade, not struggles to control markets.

Shipments of agricultural commodities and their accompanying impact on exporters and importers constitute the most important dimension of global food interdependence. While the export share of total world food production is modest—about 2 percent for all foodstuffs, and 10 percent for grains, in the recent normal year of 1976/77—food trade tends nevertheless crucially to affect the dietary well-being of both exporting and importing countries. Trade in food and agricultural products has long been important to the United States. These products constituted about 75 percent of our exports in the last part of the nineteenth century, and while this declined to about 20 percent of U.S. exports by the 1970s, America's share of total world agricultural trade has grown, and the proportion of American grain exported has also risen. Over half of all American wheat and soybeans and nearly a third of our corn and feed grain crops are sold overseas.

As table 2.1 shows, world grain trading expanded rapidly in the early 1970s, after a decade of relative stability in the 1960s. Increases in trade since 1975 can be partly accounted for by market factors such as declining prices, and some governments' attempts to build up stocks in the wake of the nearly disastrous shortages of 1972–73. But, more fundamentally, these higher trading volumes represent responses to several factors of longer-run significance. These include expanding populations in many less-developed countries, heightening affluence in OECD countries, abundances of foreign exchange in OPEC countries, strengthening economies in newly industrializing

Table 2.1 World Cereal Exports[a]

	1969/71 Average	73/74	74/75	75/76	76/77	77/78	78/79[b]
All Cereals Exported	111.2	141.6	134.8	151.1	147.3	163.6	168.4
% U.S.	35.3	54.6	47.8	52.9	53.9	53.2	54.2
Wheat	55.1	62.6	63.9	65.9	59.6	71.9	72.4
% U.S.	31.9	49.7	43.8	47.8	42.6	43.3	44.4
Coarse Grains	48.8	71.1	63.7	76.9	79.9	81.5	87.2
% U.S.	40.4	62.6	53.8	60.5	64.8	63.9	65.1
Rice	7.3	7.9	7.2	8.3	7.8	10.2	8.8[b]
% U.S.	26.0	21.5	29.2	25.0	28.2	22.5	26.1

SOURCES: For 1969/71 average, Food and Agriculture Organization, *FAO Commodity Review and Outlook*, 1975–79, Tables 6, 7, & 8; for 73/74–77/78, United States Department of Agriculture, Foreign Agricultural Service, *Foreign Agricultural Circular*, "World Grain Situation: 1977/78 Crop and Trade Developments," FG-9-77, June 13, 1977, pp. 4, 5, 10; for 78/79, FAO, *Food Outlook* (Rome: FAO, October 1979), Tables A.6 and A.7.

[a]Wheat and coarse grains for year beginning July 1; rice for calendar year.
[b]Estimated.

**Table 2.2   Net Trade in Wheat, Coarse Grain and Rice,
PRE-WAR, 1948–52, 1969–71, and 1978/79**
(in million metric tons)

Country and Region	1934–38	1948–52	1969–71	1978/79
North America	5	23	54	104
United States			(39)	(86)
Canada			(15)	(18)
Western Europe	−24	−22	−22	−14
EEC			(−17)	(−5)
Other			(−5)	(−9)
East Europe & USSR	5	–	−3	−24
Asia, Africa, Latin America	3	−6	−32	−70
Japan			(−14)	(−23)
China			(−3)	(−12)
Australia and New Zealand	3	3	11	11

SOURCES: Figures for 1934–38 and 1948–52, Lester Brown with Erik Eckholm, *By Bread Alone* (New York: Praeger, 1974), p. 61, tables 5–2; for 1969–71, Central Intelligence Agency, Directorate of Intelligence, Office of Political Research, *Potential Implications of Trends in World Population, Food Production, and Climate*, ORP-401, August 1974, Appendix I, table 4; for 1978, USDA, *World Agricultural Situation*, WAS-18, December 1978, p. 38; figures represent forecasts.

countries such as South Korea and Taiwan, and basic policy changes in the Soviet Union, several Eastern European countries, and Japan. Most projections of future demand for grain imports show substantial increases during the 1980s, even if current efforts toward self-sufficiency succeed in several countries.[3] Table 2.2 shows volumes and directions in the world's grain trade since the interwar period.

Structurally, the world's trading system has become increasingly concentrated; a few major exporters and importers dominate, more countries have become importers and there is relatively high interdependence between importers and exporters. As table 2.3 shows, most of the world's grain trade originates in North America (primarily in the United States) and Australia. In the 1960s most shipments were destined for OECD countries. By 1978 this pattern changed. The Soviet Union and China appear to have entered the market on a continuing basis, although their imports still fluctuate quite widely. A growing proportion (now about 28 percent) of the world's grain trade either originates or terminates in developing countries, especially in the form of imports to a few populous or oil-rich food-importing countries.

Concentration in the commercial system is hardly surprising in light of the facts that the unevenly distributed gifts of nature (soil and climate combined with widely different population densities) have lent only a few countries the capacity to produce agricultural surpluses necessary for market primacy, and the uneven distribution of the world's wealth has lent only a few others the financial means to meet their food needs through external purchases whenever necessary. Like other markets, the world food market responds to the selling and buying power of its participants, not to the nutritional needs of all peoples.[4] The growing reliance of the world on North American supplies of grain is illustrated in Figure 2.1.

The international commercial food market has enmeshed its participants in bonds of interdependence, but some are clearly more enmeshed than others. First, there is an asymmetry between the relative dependence of exporters and importers; the comparatively few major exporters tend to be deeply committed to commerce in foodstuffs and vulnerable to downturns in trade, whereas only some of the major importers are so critically involved. For the United States, agricultural exports in recent years have accounted annually for more than 20 percent of total export value. Earnings from agricultural sales abroad are essential elements in the U.S. balance of payments (see Table 2.4). In 1974, they rose sharply and entirely covered the petroleum deficit as well as the cost of agricultural imports. In 1977 and 1978, with trade deficits of $40 and $47 billion, agricultural trade surpluses were $10 and $13 billion respectively, covering half the costs of petroleum imports. Farming, and food processing and distribution, employ three out of ten Americans and exports contribute notably to this employment level; overseas marketing significantly lessens the costs to American taxpayers of main-

THE COMMERCIAL SYSTEM

Table 2.3   World Total Grain Production, Consumption, and Net Exports[d]
(In million metric tons)

	1960/61–62/63			1969/70–71/72		
	Pro- duction	Con- sumption	Net Exports	Pro- duction	Con- sumption	Net Exports
Developed Countries	317.6	301.9	18.9	404.0	377.6	29.9
United States	168.3	139.8	32.5	208.7	168.9	38.8
Canada	23.8	15.1	9.6	34.4	22.1	14.4
EC-9	71.5	92.0	−21.5	94.2	111.5	−16.1
Other Western Europe	20.7	24.9	−4.3	28.9	33.7	−4.9
South Africa	7.0	4.7	1.7	10.1	7.1	1.4
Japan	15.6	21.0	−5.3	12.7	27.9	−14.4
Oceania	10.8	4.4	6.2	15.0	6.3	10.8
Centrally Planned Countries	292.3	295.7	−3.4	408.7	424.1	−6.5
Eastern Europe	57.6	64.3	−6.7	75.0	83.0	−7.4
USSR	126.3	119.0	7.3	167.4	171.8	4.0
People's Republic of China	108.3	112.4	−4.0	166.2	169.3	−3.1
Developing Countries	240.5	252.2	−13.0	315.4	335.0	−20.4
Middle America	9.7	10.5	−.8	16.1	17.3	−1.0
Venezuela	.5	.9	−.4	.8	1.8	−1.0
Brazil	13.8	15.7	−2.3	20.4	22.0	−.8
Argentina	13.2	8.3	5.1	19.4	11.2	8.2
Other South America	5.6	6.7	−1.0	6.8	8.9	−2.1
North Africa/Middle East	31.7	37.0	−5.6	40.4	49.5	−9.2
Central Africa	19.0	19.8	−.8	22.5	24.3	−1.8
East Africa	7.4	7.3	.1	9.6	9.8	−.3
South Asia	92.1	97.4	−6.1	119.1	123.4	−5.1
Southeast Asia	17.3	13.4	4.0	22.9	19.8	3.3
East Asia	23.7	27.8	−4.3	30.3	37.9	−8.4
Rest of World	6.5	7.5	−.9	6.9	9.2	−2.3
Total above	850.3	849.8	—	1,128.1	1,136.8	—
World Total[a]	850.3	849.8	—	1,127.4	1,139.1	—

SOURCE: U.S. Dept. of Agriculture, *World Agricultural Situation,* WAS-18, Washington, December 1978. p. 38.

[a]World totals taken from the *September* 1978 issue of *the Foreign Agricultural on Grains.*
[b]Preliminary.
[c]Forecast.
[d]Net export figures are on a July-June basis.

Table 2.3 (Continued)

1976/77			1977/78ᵇ			1978/79ᶜ		
Pro-duction	Con-sumption	Net Exports	Pro-duction	Con-sumption	Net Exports	Pro-duction	Con-sumption	Net Exports
467.2	377.6	56.7	478.6	387.9	77.4	503.0	399.6	81.5
255.9	153.5	78.2	260.6	160.9	85.2	264.5	167.4	86.1
44.7	21.9	16.7	42.2	21.2	19.2	40.8	21.8	17.9
91.4	113.5	−22.2	104.0	115.3	−10.9	114.8	117.3	−5.0
33.4	41.9	−8.3	31.9	42.3	−9.7	36.3	44.2	−9.1
12.5	8.8	1.5	12.6	9.0	2.9	11.7	9.0	3.7
11.2	32.0	−21.4	12.5	33.1	−22.7	12.2	34.0	−23.3
18.1	6.0	12.2	14.7	6.1	13.4	22.7	5.9	11.1
506.1	514.9	−21.6	474.8	524.5	−34.8	514.8	538.6	−35.5
94.2	104.1	−11.6	93.8	104.1	−10.5	92.4	105.2	−11.8
213.2	209.8	−7.6	186.2	217.9	−16.8	220.0	218.9	−11.7
198.7	201.1	−2.4	194.9	202.4	−7.6	202.4	214.4	−12.0
379.0	397.1	−27.7	370.0	414.1	−38.2	391.0	428.0	−39.1
20.1	23.8	−2.5	18.0	24.5	−5.1	20.7	25.5	−5.1
.8	2.7	−1.8	1.5	3.2	−1.7	1.7	3.4	−1.7
27.8	28.6	−1.2	21.9	27.9	−1.9	27.7	29.6	−5.2
28.1	11.3	15.3	23.3	11.2	13.4	23.5	11.4	12.9
8.2	10.5	−2.7	7.5	10.9	−3.1	7.8	11.3	−3.4
54.7	66.1	−16.2	48.6	67.7	−19.5	53.6	70.8	−18.0
23.4	26.4	−3.4	22.8	26.6	−3.9	23.5	27.2	−3.5
10.4	10.3	−.1	10.5	10.9	−.3	10.6	11.1	−.4
133.7	137.5	−5.6	146.6	148.3	−2.7	149.2	152.9	−2.7
21.7	16.7	5.5	19.9	16.8	2.8	21.4	17.2	4.1
36.3	47.1	−12.6	36.4	50.0	−13.4	38.6	52.3	−13.4
13.7	16.1	−2.4	13.1	16.0	−2.9	12.7	15.3	−2.9
1,352.3	1,289.6	—	1,323.3	1,326.4	—	1,408.8	1,366.2	—
1,352.6	1,297.8	—	1,322.3	1,329.7	—	1,408.8	1,366.8	—

taining farm incomes in this country. Much the same is true for the other major food exporters; Canada exports approximately 35 percent of its agricultural output yearly and Australia exports 70 percent.⁵ In both countries, overseas sales contribute significantly to both farm income (33 percent for Canada and 50 percent for Australia in 1976), and to balance-of-payments equilibrium, and for both

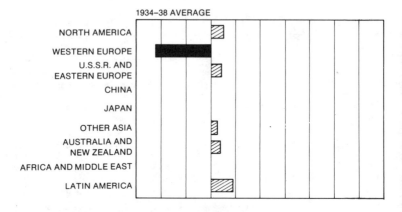

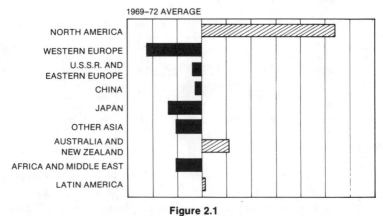

Figure 2.1
Net Grain Trade and Growing World Dependence upon North America

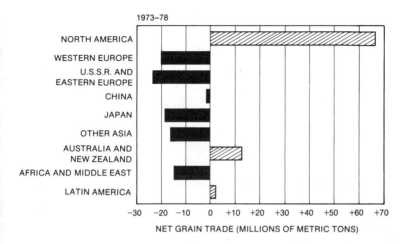

The world's increasing dependence on grain exports of a few countries is shown by this comparison of the trade pattern before World War II with the situation more recently and estimated figures for 1975/76. Data are from Lester R. Brown, the Department of Agriculture, and IFPRI. Before the war most regions exported grain (pattern): Western Europe imported it (solid). Now, the U.S. and Canada supply most of the grain to make up deficits.

SOURCE: U.S. Dept. of Agriculture, "International Food Policy Issues, A Proceedings," January 1978, p. 15.

Figure 2.1 (Continued)

countries downturns on the international market generate critical economic and political problems of adjustment, as they do in the United States.[6]

Among importers, Japan and the countries of the European Communities buy most heavily on the world market. Imports into the EC consist mainly of feed grains consumed by animals raised for meat and dairy purposes. Russian purchases in recent years have been largely for similar purposes. Japan's imports are high and directed in greater measure to immediate human consumption, and the situation is similar for the imports of the OPEC countries and some of the newly industrializing countries. All of these countries

Table 2.4   U.S. Agricultural Trade Balance
1971/72–1978/79

	Year beginning October 1							
	1971/72	1972/73	1973/74	1974/75	1975/76	1976/77	1977/78	Forecast 1978/79
	Dollars Billion							
Exports	8.24	14.98	21.61	21.85	22.76	24.00	27.30	30.3
Imports	5.94	7.74	10.06	9.47	10.51	13.38	13.89	14.8
Trade balance	2.30	7.24	11.55	12.38	12.25	10.62	13.42	15.5
	Million Metric Tons							
Export volume	60.7	99.7	93.4	87.2	106.7	102.2	121.7	121.9

SOURCE: Outlook for U.S. Agricultural Exports (Washington, USDA, February 16, 1979), p.2.

command strong foreign-exchange positions; thus they can, and are likely to, continue to purchase internationally even under tight market conditions (barring sellers' embargoes, of course). Therefore most of the major buyers of food internationally might be described as dependent upon the world food market, but rather invulnerable to its vagaries. Western Europeans and Russians chose to exercise little "belt tightening" during recent international shortages, in spite of diets that allowed them to do so, and almost all the larger importers have the exchange resources to absorb the high prices of tight markets for extended periods of time. By striking contrast, the less-developed countries, including China, import mainly in order to fulfill human needs. They have almost no "belt tightening" options and possess meager exchange reserves. Therefore they are both dependent upon the international market and highly vulnerable to its upward fluctuations. In sum, while *interdependence* accurately de-scribes the commercial system for food, such interdependence tends to be asymmetric and bargaining power among buyers and sellers under varying market conditions tends to reflect these asymmetries. (Table 2.5 shows the proportion of trade related to production of exporters and consumption of importers.)

As noted in chapter 1, the world food market has been subject to wide fluctuations in prices in recent years. After more than two

**Table 2.5   Stakes of Major Participants in
International Grain Trade**

Major Exporters	Cereals Exports as % of Total Cereals Production (By Weight, 1973-75 Average)
Australia	51.5
Canada	43.2
Argentina	41.3
France	39.2
United States	33.1

Major Importers	Cereals Imports as % of Total Cereals Consumption (By Weight, 1973-75 Average)
Belgium-Luxembourg	89.6
Japan	53.5
United Kingdom	34.8
Italy	33.6
Egypt	27.6
West Germany	27.4
South Korea	26.8
Spain	24.3
Bangladesh	16.3
Brazil	9.9
Soviet Union	8.6
India	4.5
China	2.0[a]

SOURCES: Based on data published by Henry Nau in "The Diplomacy of World Food: Goals, Capabilities, Issues and Arenas," in Hopkins and Puchala, eds., *The Global Political Economy of Food* (Madison: University of Wisconsin Press, 1978), p. 209; figures for China computed from data published in USDA, *World Agricultural Situation,* WAS-18, December 1978, p. 38.

[a]For years 1969-72.

decades of relative stability in the 1950s and 1960s, during which average grain export prices seldom varied by more than a few percentage points from year to year, the 1970s saw dramatic price shifts, as for example the 400 percent increase in American wheat export prices between 1972 and 1974, followed by the 200 percent decline between

1974 and 1977.[7] These fluctuations are the results of changing supply conditions, some idiosyncratic alterations in demand, and some fundamental revisions in stock-holding policies in the United States and Canada.[8] After the deliberate drawing down of American and Canadian stocks in 1973, there were no appreciable reserves to alleviate the combined impacts of widespread crop damage and massive Russian buying. Nor, in the absence of stock-accumulating policies in the United States and elsewhere, was it possible to buffer the rapid depression of the market that began after the plentiful harvests of 1975. When all is said, however, the most important observations on the unstable market focus neither on its description nor its causes, but on its impacts. Market instability lends unpredictability to commercial dealings, renders macroeconomic planning inaccurate and unhelpful in both exporting and importing countries, impairs development in less-developed countries, raises inflammatory political issues, and alternatively highly rewards the rich and greatly penalizes the poor both within and between countries. Reasonable and regular price fluctuations tend to enhance economic efficiency; extreme and erratic ones undermine it.

The final point to be made in describing the world food market is that it is rather imperfect, not only in the inordinate power of a few big sellers and buyers (the economist's oligopolies and oligopsonies), but in the extraordinarily high degree of governmental intervention into food and agricultural affairs, both production and marketing, in exporting and importing countries. As Henry Nau points out,

All of the major grain exporters except the United States operate through centralized boards of grain trade. . . . In the United States, grain sales are subject to export control legislation and since 1975 to stricter export reporting requirements. . . . Major importing countries also centralize grain trade. In Japan, an import agency monopolizes grain purchases. In the Soviet Union and China, state trading agencies dominate. And in the EEC import levies, like export subsidies, are set by the Community and administered by national authorities. India, Bangladesh and many other developing countries also employ central trading organizations.[9]

The regulation of food trade is not improper. Indeed, quite to the contrary, when it is apparent that unregulated markets are antithetical to nutritional adequacy and economic equity, intervention is in order. Nonetheless, widespread trade distortion does follow from various countries' attempts to either isolate their domestic agriculture from world markets, or to exploit the world market to national advantage in mercantilistic fashion. Evidence demonstrates that such trade-distorting practices compound inefficiencies in the use of agronomic resources, encourage inappropriate crop mixes, penalize consumers, hamper structural reform in agriculture and, perhaps most deleterious of all, deter rural modernization and economic development.[10] As might be expected, the greatest economic harm in such practices tends to fall most readily and most heavily upon the poorest

Table 2.6   Estimated Producer-Subsidy Values by Countries and Commodities, 1968–74

	1968	1969	1970	1971	1972	1973	1974
Total producer-subsidy values (in U.S. $)							
Australia	394	391	349	368	386	356	79
Canada	774	809	872	951	865	857	845
EEC	8,374	8,706	7,355	6,231	5,590	3,193	−559
Japan	4,002	4,278	4,988	4,828	6,316	8,711	6,804
United Kingdom	749	798	798	853	722	530	317
United States	5,969	6,926	7,069	5,702	5,433	5,281	5,155
Total	20,262	21,908	21,431	18,933	19,312	18,928	12,641
Wheat	2,090	2,507	2,465	2,711	2,665	−1,177	−1,710
Barley	661	936	634	922	718	125	−286
Maize	1,661	1,825	1,641	1,516	2,006	1,086	99
Rice	3,822	4,090	4,857	4,753	6,221	8,519	6,427
Sugar	2,334	2,019	1,926	2,051	1,677	1,492	−2,371
Dairy	9,694	10,531	9,909	6,980	6,024	8,883	10,482
Total	20,262	21,908	21,431	18,933	19,312	18,928	12,641

SOURCE: FAO, Agricultural Protection and Stabilization Policies: A Framework of Measurement in the Context of Agricultural Adjustment (Rome: Food and Agriculture Organization, October 1975), Table V.3.

people in the poorest countries. Therefore, quite apart from the philosophical debates between the economic "liberals" and "interventionists" there is something to be said for examining trade distortions empirically for their immediate and longer-term impacts on global food security.[11] Table 2.6 shows subsidies applied by various governments on sales between 1968 and 1974. Notice, in particular, the high subsidies applied for the purpose of moving exports during periods of abundance (1968 and 1969) and the taxes applied, notably by the EEC, to discourage trade during periods of scarcity (1974). Market cues are obviously distorted under such conditions.

Goals Served by
the Commercial Food System

Fundamentally speaking, the international food market distributes agricultural commodities from producers to consumers, as it directs the movements of commodities from countries and regions where local supplies surpass demands to areas where demands surpass supplies. Moreover, by its pricing effect, it provides cues to governments and individuals as to prospective gains from increasing inputs in food production or from shifting them elsewhere. Admittedly, the supply and demand of the "market" are measured in terms of capacity and preference for exchange and not in terms of human needs, as critics of the "inequities" in the international market frequently note. Their points are well taken. However, criticizing biases of the international market for favoring wealthy consumers who eat well, while others languish near starvation, should not overwhelm discussion of the functions it does perform and the goals it serves rather well.

In the most general sense, the market, the more it is undominated and integrated, is to be credited for efficiently performing the allocative function of matching supply to demand. Under normal conditions, and in the context of accurate and rapidly flowing information, price movements and profit results will guide production for the market and not only shift distribution and consumption in a "rational" fashion, but also provide a basis for moving the bulk of the world's commodities without centralized direction or elaborate administrative control. Given the decentralized structure of international politics, the obvious domestic political obstacles to supranational regulation and allocation, and the monumental administrative task that would be involved in running a fully "administered" exchange, it is difficult to imagine, and foolish to advocate, a world food system without a world food market. Realistic policy discussions should be directed not toward eliminating the market but toward "perfecting" it by moderating its excesses, reducing obstacles and barriers, and compensating for biases.

The value of the commercial system to the major food exporters was obvious from previous discussion. As noted before, for the United States, in particular, the ability and profitability in marketing agricultural surpluses has helped to generate high and rising farm incomes (exports account for approximately 8 percent of GNP contributed by the U.S. farm sector) and food production and processing, also linked to exports, account for employment of more than a quarter of the American labor force. Exchange earnings from food sales abroad are crucial in the United States balance of payments, and during several years in the 1970s such sales have been the single largest credit entry on our external accounts.

In addition, the orientation of American agriculture, especially encouraged by farm legislation in 1973—where U.S. prices were rendered much more dependent upon international supply/demand relationships than they had been—contributes to sizable savings in the costs of domestic farm-support programs (at least when international demand is high), eliminates other costly public interventions into the farm sector, and generally eases the burdens upon taxpayers that our agricultural policies impose. While there is no way to accurately gauge the extent to which export programs have impacted upon political stability, since rural discontent is traditional in American politics and rather invariant over time, it can at least be suggested that political crises stemming from severe price depression are inversely correlated with thriving sales abroad. The farm protests of 1977 were the first since the farm depression of 1923 which could be said to stem directly from the effects of lower prices in world markets. Related pressures protesting massive public interventions to support falling prices are also less likely in the context of healthy export markets. Generally speaking, political problems originating in rural America mount when export markets sag, as in 1976. To show that agricultural exports serve a range of goals in Canada, Australia, Argentina (and France, Holland, and Denmark) quite similar to those served in the United States would be to belabor an obvious point. The world market well serves exporters' economic and political aims, especially when the market remains a sellers' arena, as it has through much of the 1970s, when the U.S. leadership spoke of "food power" and U.S. farmers had higher incomes than the urban populace for the first time in recent history.

Importers' economic, social, and political aims are also bound up with the international food market. Food imports into industrial countries serve largely to provide variety and richness in diet beyond basic nutritional needs. As noted, the Western Europeans and Russians enter the international market to meet their feed grain needs, and to increase thereby their animal-product consumption. To a certain extent the Japanese do likewise. Analysts sensitive to problems of world hunger have taken feed-grain importers to task for their behavior and branded their goals "overconsumption."[12] Be this as it may, affluence tends to be as much reflected in diet as in other aspects of the quality of life, and it is hardly likely that the wealthier peoples of the world will abandon their eating habits or their demands upon the international market to support them. Beyond the nutritional goals served by food imports into industrialized countries, such purchases also serve macroeconomic ends. Exploiting efficiencies resulting from an international division of labor and buying at lowest prices, for example, serves as an anti-inflationary tool in food-importing countries. Importing, instead of developing high-cost agriculture, also saves investment capital and contributes to faster growth. As a case in point, the short-lived Japanese drive for 75 percent self-sufficiency after the shocks of 1973/74 proved costly beyond all expectation, and the Japanese soon returned to seeking import security instead of plowing their parks and ball fields.[13] In all of these situations, political implications are linked to economic outcomes. Few Western governments, and indeed probably not even the Soviet government, could easily politically weather having to constrain greatly the dietary affluence of their citizens. Few, likewise, can politically afford to overlook the positive relationships between low-cost food and national economic growth.

Except for the few countries where food imports are used to buttress rapid industrialization directly, as in South Korea and some OPEC countries, most Third World importers count upon international purchases (or aid as discussed in chapter 3) to keep per capita food intake at minimally adequate levels. Such, for example, has been the goal of Indian food-import policy, and it is presently probably the Chinese goal as well. For some LDC buyers the international market is a means toward preventing widespread starvation, and many of these countries, particularly in South Asia, look to a long run of larger international purchases. For others, the capacity to procure supplies internationally serves a stopgap end in feeding populations until local agriculture can be modernized and greater self-sufficiency attained. Brazil appears to be such a case. It is also true that for still others, perhaps India in the 1950s, the availability of international supplies provides the excuse to delay local rural reform. After the pressures of the early 1970s, and especially in light of events in Ethiopia, Upper Volta, Egypt, Bangladesh, Niger, and elsewhere in hungry countries, there is no question that food scarcity easily links to turmoil and violence in the fragile politics of the Third World.[14]

Therefore, to the extent that food imports alleviate critical scarcities, such imports are directly linked to political stability.

Issues and Problems in Food Trade

Despite the ends it serves for exporters and importers, the functioning of the international commercial system for food remains problematic. The current agenda of policy problems includes (1) the general issue of price stability, and, specifically, related questions of reserves and adjustment mechanisms; (2) the general issue of trade liberalization, and the more particular questions of importers' restrictions and exporters' subsidies and embargoes; and (3) the general issue of market biases against poor countries, and the specific questions of special treatment for LDC exports and attention to their basic human needs.

Market Stability and Adjustment Mechanisms

While there is presently a debate concerning solutions to these problems, most analysts agree that the propensity to extreme and erratic price instability on the international grain market is a condition of major concern.[15] All but the most committed of the laissez faire school find extreme instability undesirable and "free market" adjustment inadequate. Such adjustment frequently results in overreaction, which exacerbates cycles of instability (or at least perpetuates them), or else it is limited by policy in some countries where marketing is constrained by official controls; the result is that a greater burden is placed on other countries and adjustments to changing international conditions are slowed.

Policy frameworks for responding to problems of price instability reflect the range of their causes. To the extent that international price fluctuations stem from variations in supply, inevitable to some extent as a result of weather or other environmental causes, as argued in chapter 1, the obvious response is counter-cyclically to accumulate and release buffer stocks in quantities sufficient to moderate prices without destroying their utility as cues to production and consumption. The idea of reserve stocks is traditional and simple. Indeed American and Canadian national reserves (plus Russian belt-tightening in 1963 in lieu of massive importing) accounted for the relative stability of international grain prices through most of the 1960s. The problem is that all three countries were driven by motives unrelated to stability—the U.S. and Canada to manipulate domestic farm prices, and the Soviet Union to avoid heavy foreign expenditures. None of these countries follow the same policies in the 1970s.

The issue about reserves at present concerns not the principle of buffering, however, but the problem of competing philosophies of agricultural management and of who should "pay." The United Nations proposed in 1974 that stocks should be nationally held (in deference to political and financial reality) but that governments should "cooperate in ensuring the availability at all times of adequate cereal supplies in the world."[16] As unanimously recommended by the 1974 World Food Conference, at a minimum such cooperation must involve agreement upon desirable magnitudes of stocks; agreement upon guidelines for the timing of accumulation and release of national stocks, and appropriate triggers; agreement upon the extent and specificity of national obligations to import and export during buffering phases; agreement upon information and consultation required to manage grain stocks internationally; and agreement upon institutions required to internationally coordinate national decisions regarding stocks. In addition, poor-country participants have sought special help to meet their costs of holding stocks in a reserve system. Negotiations for a reserve—opened formally in the fall of 1975—collapsed in February, 1979, with seeming intractable differences over the size of the reserve. Neither could a final compromise be reached over prices at which stocks would be released and acquired, and less-developed countries remained dissatisfied with the lack of concession in the terms generally. Stalemate in the grain-reserve negotiations in 1979 occurred despite American willingness to broadly increase its food-aid commitment and to split differences with the European position.

The impulse to seek international solutions to instability of food prices and farm incomes in major trading countries has a history that dates back to a Wheat Executive (1916–19) and to discussions on price cooperation at the International Economic Conference in Geneva in 1927. Agricultural interests, faced with large crops in 1926, then sought to share in the rising world propserity by proposing international cooperation on wheat matters.[17] Nothing came of these talks. But five years later, in response to the desperation of worldwide depression, and as a result of no less than twenty conferences on wheat problems, the first International Wheat Agreement was reached among 22 countries meeting in London in August, 1933. For the next 2 years the major exporters—Argentina, Australia, Canada and the United States—agreed to cut exports by 15 percent and to cut their crop acreage correspondingly. Eastern European countries, and even the Soviet Union, also agreed to limit exports. Importers agreed to lower custom duties and not to expand production; prices were expected to be stabilized. Although the agreement had all the essentials of a commodity-management regime—supply regulations, export controls, and price provisions—it failed. American and Canadian policy makers never made required acreage reductions, though a drought had that effect. Bumper crops led Argentina to break the agreement on its share of exports, and importers maintained barriers (in some countries including a requirement that up to 100 percent of wheat milled be of national origin) in the face of declining world prices.[18] Over the next five years, the only component of the 1933 agreement to work was the secretariat it called for—the Wheat Advisory Committee. However, the massive surpluses of the early depression years receded, so that even though human consumption dropped 5 percent per capita worldwide by 1938, prices were rising. Concern over bumper crops that year, which led to a doubling of world carry-over stocks and a decline in prices,[19] led to negotiations for a new agreement. This was reached but never signed because of the outbreak of World War II.

During the war years, the Wheat Advisory Committee became the International Wheat Council, but the agreement that it worked on in 1942 never received much attention due to the priority of war efforts and the major dislocations in production at the time. It had proposed a sharing of markets among major traders—16 percent for the United States, 40 percent for Canada, 19 percent for Argentina, and 25 percent for Australia.

A draft treaty presented in 1948 was not ratified by the United States, then in the throes of an election campaign, but a new effort in 1949 succeeded. The International Wheat Agreement of 1949, reached at a conference in Washington, called for minimum tonnage guarantees by importers and price-range guarantees by exporters. Eventually, 46 countries adhered to the 4-year agreement, which was renewed in 1952 and 1956. At first, the Agreement worked well as surplus stocks were low, European demand was high, and transactions under the Agreement were well below the world open-market price. In effect grain exporters, increasingly the United States and Canada, subsidized sales to importers in exchange for promises to buy at least stipulated minimum quantities. As surpluses increased in 1952, and thereafter, prices fell to within the negotiated ranges and importers reduced *both* their formal obligations and their actual purchases under the treaty. Table 2.7 summarizes transactions under the 1949–1956 Agreements.

By 1959, importers balked at any fixed requirements, and agreements in 1959, 1962, and extensions through 1967, merely said that a minimum percentage of imports had to come from IWA members (but importers could choose to import any amount). Prices remained very stable during this period, as figure 2.2 shows, but not because of the agreement. The control of prices was due to the willingness of the United States and Canada "to engage themselves in

Table 2.7   Transactions under International Wheat Agreements, 1949–1959
(Transactions guaranteed and recorded)

Year	Guaranteed Quantity (Million Metric Tons)	Guaranteed Price Range ($ per bushel)	Recorded Transactions As % of Guaranteed	Recorded Transactions As % of World Trade	Price Per Bushel
1949/50	14.3	1.50–1.80	83	51	1.99–2.31
50/51	15.3	1.50–1.80	94	57	
51/52	15.6	1.50–1.80	100	54	
52/53	15.8	1.50–1.80	99	66	
53/54	10.6	1.55–2.05	58	25	Within
54/55	10.7	1.55–2.05	74	28	Range
55/56	10.7	1.55–2.05	64	24	
56/57	8.0	1.50–2.00	73	16	
57/58	8.0	1.50–2.00	66	16	
58/59	8.0	1.50–2.00	65	15	

SOURCE: International Wheat Agreements: A Historical and Critical Background (London: International Wheat Council, 1974) pp. 28–40. Document EX/(74/75) 2/2.

supply management and export pricing,"[20] They controlled 60 percent to 70 percent of world trade and held 80 percent to 90 percent of stocks. Given the policies they used to manage their domestic farm economies, they were induced to also manage international trade. Indeed, the Soviet Union, which joined the IWA in 1962 as an exporter, was unable to distort prices despite unexpected imports of nine million metric tons of wheat in 1963 because stocks were so high. The price band of the agreement was thus maintained by exporter collaboration, induced by large stocks.

The 1967 Agreement continued the minimum price of $1.50 per bushel, but exporting countries had commonly begun to shift their domestic farm policies. Minimum international prices were not maintained, domestic prices were kept low, and the political conditions for moving policy from price supports to income supports for farmers (as used in the United Kingdom prior to EEC membership) were being laid. In September 1969, world prices were well below minimum, and importers showed insufficient interest in paying higher prices and thus did not act to raise prices to the minimum

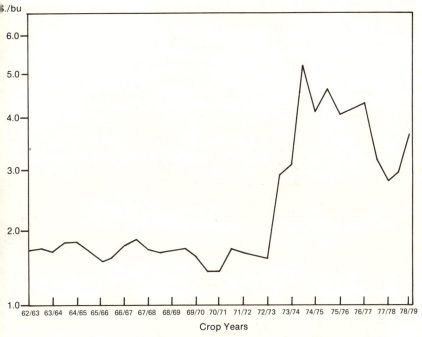

SOURCE: USDA, *The World Food Situation and Prospects to 1985* (U.S. Dept. of Agriculture: Washington, D.C., 1 19), p. 25, for years 1962–1972.

Figure 2.2
The Trend in Wheat Prices[a] 1962/63–1977/78

[a]US No. 2 Hard Red Winter, fob Gulf

agreed. While exporters had subsidized importers when market prices were at $2.00 or better above those of the Agreement in 1949–53, importers did not subsidize exporters in 1969 at the $1.50 minimum. Confusion over having many different prices for various wheat varieties contributed to the problem of importer accountability, but this was not central to it. Rather, it was a case of opportunistic deviation from the international agreement, and the result was the demise of the Agreement's main provisions.

Since 1969 there have been no effective price provisions, stocking provisions, supply controls, or trading rules in the international wheat economy, although the IWC continues to monitor trade. Exporters and importers continued consultations on a new agreement from 1970 onwards and worked within the IWC as an important consultative vehicle. Basically since 1971 the old agreements have been renewed without price provisions.

Especially since 1975, continuing negotiations for a new agreement—one which would include provisions for world food security—have repeated the movement of issues and calculations of advantage familiar in earlier periods as shifts from excess supply to scarcity occur. In 1975, UN and American officials suggested that an international grain reserve of 30 million metric tons of wheat would be of adequate size to buffer foreseeable price fluctuations, and stocks of this magnitude should also dampen disruptive speculation and hoarding. Coarse grains might be added to the reserve later. The Food and Agriculture Organization has calculated that stores amounting to approximately 17 percent to 18 percent of yearly consumption represent a minimum safe ratio for world food security. These are currently in existence, with stocks at 19 percent in 1978/79. They are, however, concentrated in private hands in Western countries, and not committed or orchestrated to purposes of international market stabilization. They are not an adequate global food reserve.

As to issues of triggering, the 1977 American shift to accept the positions of the European Communities on the question of price rather than quantity triggers was not a costly compromise of United States interests. The problem is agreeing on a high enough growth range and then gaining a commitment from the EC to buy at "floor" prices for market stabilization purposes regardless of internal prices in the Communities. Understandably, too, there must be a European agreement to curtail imports and perhaps increase exports when shortages drive prices to their "ceilings." An additional attribute of a price trigger system is that the information required for its effective operation is less extensive and more rapidly and readily available than that which would be required for a "quantity triggered" system.[21] At a minimum, however, any triggering mechanism demands a free and rapid flow of information, plus regularly assembled forums for international consultation and decision, as have begun to emerge in the multinational trading firms and in increased collaboration among the government bureaucracies of the biggest trading countries.

As noted, negotiations toward a new grains agreement failed in February, 1979. The old agreement was extended to 1981 and parties to the negotiations agreed that this extension should not prejudice chances for a new agreement before 1981. The impasse can be blamed on a variety of pressures and competing understandings among negotiators, but most notably on the fact that importers were not motivated to contribute to the creation of international stocks during a period of falling prices and poor countries objected to proposed prices in 1979 that seemed high to them. We know historically that grains agreements have been seriously sought most often in times of surpluses, but that the provisions of these agreements have never worked, as in 1933 and 1967. The 1949 agreement anticipated falling prices and rising stocks, but when this did not occur, the agreement— abetted by demands of the Korean War and the holding of modest stocks off the market by exporters—seemed to work. But, in all cases, circumstances external to the provisions of the agreements and adherence to them by governments shaped outcomes in grain markets. National governments can, and do, control the production and marketing of grain within their domains. International organizations and agreements do not and have not. However, models for conditions under which greater international regulation will work clearly exist, for example when the world economy is dominated by a single force, as was the case with the United States from 1946 to 1955, or when oligopoly works to the advantage of buyers, as in the U.S.-Canadian-managed international grain market of the 1960s.

Ideally, an international-reserve facility should require (1) the participation of all major producing and consuming countries (notably including the USSR, whose abstention could seriously weaken the mechanism); (2) liaison with the large grain-trading companies; and (3) clear rules for action by the international committees, secretariat, and responsible member governments whenever upper or lower price targets are approached. There is no question that the grain reserves should be internationally managed, not because "internationalism" itself is a noble ideal, but because any alternative stocking practices result either in countries manipulating reserves in their own domestic political or economic interest—which usually will be to the detriment of stability on the international market if national and international interest conflict—or in one or a few countries unilaterally bearing market-adjustment burdens for the world. The cost of American-Canadian international grain management was imposed heavily upon taxpayers during periods of oversupply, and upon consumers during periods of short supply. American reluctance to reassume unilaterally this adjustment and stabilization burden in the grain negotiations of 1975–79 is understandable. There is hope yet for an international agreement on grains in the 1980s, since market conditions could bring coincidence in exporters' needs for stability and importers' concerns for security. But if global agreement on a regime for grains proves impossible, the United States should seek, in collaboration with other exporters bilateral arrangements with importers in order to move at least part of the way toward food security with market stability.

Market instability caused by shifts in supply due to changing crop conditions tends at times to be exacerbated, as we have noted, by artificial constraints on volumes of commodities flowing in international commerce. The notorious American Soybean Embargo in 1973 is an obvious case in point, though the less publicized acts of the European Communities imposing export taxes on grains during the same period of international shortage also had deleterious effects on world prices. As politically enticing as such behavior might be in solving national inflationary problems at the expense of the world, their shorter-term national benefits must be weighed against the longer-term damage inflicted upon exporters' credibility. For example, the United States may have lost a significant part of its market for soybeans in Japan. As a result of Japan's investments in Brazil (in the interest of import security), Brazilian soybeans moved in a few years to take a fifth of the world market. There is no need to belabor the point; the obvous postcript to any call for international management in the interest of price stability is the reminder that unilateral self-control is also very much in order.

Finally, in recent years, and especially between 1972 and 1974, unpredictable and harmful price fluctuations followed after rapid and massive Soviet interventions into the international grain market. Russian behavior is also characterized by unpredictable, precipitous withdrawals. As a result of the Soviet ability to disrupt the international market (and others' potential to do this as well) by shifting demand abruptly, measures to manage prices must include devices to control such behavior. A long-term purchasing agreement with the USSR is presently in effect as a means toward controlling erratic demand. But it does not substitute for thorough and responsible Russian intergration into the international grain market, does not constrain Russian dealings with other major exporters, does not effectively control possible transshipments, and does not broach the secrecy about Soviet crop conditions or agricultural policy which makes Russian trading "unpredictable."[22] Policing Russian behavior through marketing agreements should certainly continue (though creating too many such agreements with numerous countries is not advisable, since it can inject too much inflexibility into the market—especially if a large reserve is not in place.) But the thrust of policy efforts should be directed toward attempting to bring forth from Moscow more appreciation of the interdependence of the world food system and more cooperation in managing it by continuing and expanding the 1973 and 1975 agreements and the semiannual consultations of senior agricultural officials, as well as by edging the Russians toward greater participation in international food organizations, as discusssed in chapter 5.

Liberalizing Trade in Agricultural Commodities

The object in seeking to liberalize international agricultural trade is to exploit efficiencies in comparative advantage to attain highest production and consumption at lowest cost in resources. This object is desirable, especially when it means lower prices to consumers and improvements in diets as a result (though it seldom in fact means this directly). Obstacles to freeing trade lie in the political risks or losses of groups and interests that gain economically from the insulation of national markets. Therefore, the fundamental task in freeing trade presently is to bring about the reform of national agricultural policies that abet protectionism. Notably, no major participants in the international market are presently willing to consider this task in spite of much talk about the principles of free trade.

At issue in agricultural relations between the United States (and other exporters) and the European Communities is the structure and functioning of the EC's Common Agricultural Policy (CAP). The Treaty Establishing the European Economic Community signed at Rome in 1958 contained nine articles dealing with agriculture and looking to a community-wide farm policy as an integral element of European economic integration.[23] Aims of the new agricultural regime were to increase production and productivity, to insure fair standards of living and acceptable incomes to farmers, to stabilize markets and secure food supplies, and to provide reasonable prices to consumers. By 1962, EEC member states achieved agreement in principle that their approach to a common agricultural policy would be "to create a special agency which would not only set up rules and regulations but fix prices and provide a marketing system, with all that the term implies, for various commodities. [This would] mean establishing common prices, common support levels, and a system for unrestricted movement of agricultural products within the [then] Six. A common marketing system also implied a common tariff in trade with countries outside the Market."[24] Europe's CAP emerged in phases between 1962 and 1972 with agreements and intracommunity adjustments on fats and oils in 1966; cereals, rice, pork, poultry products, and sugar in 1967; beef, veal, and dairy products in 1968; wine, tobacco, flax, and hemp in 1970; and fruits and vegetables in 1972.[25] The common market in agriculture, with an open trade in agricultural commodities was formally established by agreement of the Ministers of Agriculture of the Six in June, 1967.

To explore the workings of the CAP in great detail would be beside the point of this analysis since our concern is with the external effects of the European regime and with American-European relations in food trade. Nonetheless, the logic and some of the workings of the CAP must be demonstrated in order to show the rationale behind the EC's external policies concerning agricultural commodities. First, and perhaps most significant, the establishment of the European Common Market to a certain extent represented an international bargain between France and West Germany: French agriculture was to gain unfettered access to the promising German market, and German industry would gain the French market.[26] Therefore, a common market for agriculture was a *sine qua non* for European intergration. But though West German agriculture was high-cost and comparatively inefficient, it could not be completely sacrificed upon the altar of European unity, because farm interests within Germany, and within the Christian Democratic Party in particular, would not allow this. It therefore became imperative that prices on the Common Market should be relatively high, closer to German than to French ones, yet neither so high as to deny French farmers an expanding market in Germany, nor so low as to drive German farmers into desperation en masse. A structural reform as anticipated under the Mansholt Plan would eventually solve the problem of high-cost, inefficient farming in Germany and elsewhere in the Community, or, at least so it was believed,[27] but until such reform was completed, high food prices would be the rule within the EEC. Aside from what the "high price" policies negotiated in 1964 implied internally, with the penalties they meted out to consumers and the competitive disadvantages they posed for low-cost producers like the Dutch, externally they implied that the European Communities had to be insulated against penetration from low-cost producers in third countries, immediately from the Danes, and especially from the Americans and Canadians.[28] Had the EEC permitted its markets to be deluged from the outside, the Franco-German cement holding the integrating European edifice together would have been greatly weakened.

Second—and technically important—because commodity prices under the CAP are politically set (and set high) rather than economically determined in the marketplace, authorities in Brussels must constantly employ a range of instruments to manage supply in efforts to maintain approximate supply-demand equilibrium at regulated prices. The principal means of managing supplies, which tend to run into surpluses under high-price incentives to farmers and disincentives to consumers, is a commitment to public purchases and stock-holding by EC authorities. Ironically, commitments to accumulate stocks during times of oversupply were written into the CAP with the expectation that managing supply in this way would be least costly to governments' treasuries (and ultimately to taxpayers) because surpluses were unlikely to occur in agricultures which traditionally produced well short of self-sufficiency. Of course this has not been the case under the CAP, where 90 percent self-sufficiency has been attained, where surpluses have been generated in nearly everything except feed grains and oil seeds, where the Communities are net exporters of butter, poultry, wheat, beef, and a number of products formerly imported, and where the cost to national treasuries for supporting the CAP's public-purchase commitments has risen astronomically. Again, the internal implications of this are manifold and revealing as regards the politics and economics of European integration, as for example in mounting West German concerns about paying the bill for the CAP, in British concerns about high food prices despite huge surpluses, and in the European Commission's concerns about further "food mountains" that will follow upon the almost certain accession of Spain, Portugal, and Greece. But, more relevant to this study, the CAP's supply-management system further necessitates insulating the internal food markets of the EEC from penetration by third countries, for low-priced imports cannot be allowed to create or contribute to internal surpluses that Community authorities would then be compelled to purchase at high prices and at European taxpayers' expense. In addition, the accumulation of large stocks in the interest of supply management within the EEC also prompts Brussels to promote exports vigorously sometimes by using internationally questionable procedures, which have become sources of diplomatic dispute.

Two EC practices in particular are highly questionable. First, most commodities that might compete with domestically produced products are subjected to variable tariff levies under the CAP, roughly equivalent to the difference between domestic producers' prices and those of external suppliers. In effect, this means that price competition from abroad is impossible, and that foreign produce may enter only after internal markets are cleared (generally at prices well above world market ones, except during 1973–75). Furthermore, as politically determined internal prices, that must invariably be high, since consensus among the Nine can usually be reached only by "bargaining up," encourage greater (albeit uneconomic) production in Western Europe, the external regime of the CAP more or less guarantees that ever-diminishing proportions of internal consumption will be accounted for by imports. (See table 2.2 for projected declines in EC import demand.) Second, and also at issue, is the EC's rather unabashed use of export subsidies, or "restitution payments" to move surplus commodities out of the Nine and onto third-country markets in direct competition with the marketing efforts of Americans, Canadians and others. Since surpluses in some commodities accumulate rapidly, and sometimes massively, in the European Communities as a result of CAP commitments to stabilize internal prices through public purchases, "restitution payments" are looked upon within as safety-valve measures for managing stocks. Externally, of course, they are looked upon as international dumping.

The Western European position in international agricultural negotiations is not inflexible, though it is very different from the American position. EC negotiators are preoccupied with the notion of "stable markets," and this, for them, means organized, administratively regulated markets highly insulated against vagaries and unpredictabilities. In effect, they look to an international regime that approximates the globalization of the CAP.[29] They have not absolutely limited access to their markets, but they offer it only under administratively guarded conditions in the context of commodity arrangements for the "main products which are essential for human consumption" (cereals, rice, sugar, and milk products).[30] These arrangements would include price bands, preferential purchase and supply obligations, and coordinated stockpiles. Trading in other products would be subject to "concerted disciplines," or rules of good conduct, between exporters and importers; and, where possible and sensible within the overall frameworks of domestic agricultural policy and foreign economic policy, reciprocal tariff reductions could be entertained. For its part, the United States is preoccupied with abolishing "unfair" trade practices in agriculture, with exposing and eliminating nontariff barriers in the food trade, and with expanding exports via predictable gains from general liberalization. In short, "freeing" markets is of much greater interest to the United States than "organizing" them. In many respects US-EC negotiations about agricultural trade amount to the respective parties talking past rather than to one another.

Criticizing the EC's Common Agricultural Policy and calling for its revision with regard to variable levies and restitution payments have been central ingredients in United States negotiating positions from the Kennedy Round to the present. While there is merit in American arguments, there is also apparent futility in making them, for Brussels is unlikely to compromise. For one thing the Europeans look upon challenges to the CAP as foreign interventions into internal matters. Here the European perceptions are comparable to what might be the case in Washington, and on Capitol Hill in particular, if a foreign power were to exert pressure to gain influence over United States farm policy—e.g., decisions on set asides, loan and target rates, and the like. This is not necessarily to suggest that the situations *are* comparable; it is only to note that they may very well look that way to Europeans. In addition, the CAP as a symbol of European integration remains meaningful and important to the Nine. But even more important is the interlocked structure of political compromises among Nine governments and hundreds of agricultural groups and thousands of local farm leaders that originally created the CAP, to say nothing of the pride, influence, and understandable obstinacy of the bureaucratic architects and executives directly and personally responsible for farm policy in Europe.[31]

In light of the probable continuation of the CAP, and in lieu of U.S. willingness to accept the EC's regime of "organized" marketing in exchange for greater access, appropriate American goals in trade dealings with the EC should be to reduce aspirations, tone down philosophical questioning, and seek reciprocities on the few practical issues where improved relationships might be made. It would seem, for example, that mutual concessions might be bargained on dairy products, where both the U.S. and the EC protect local production to exorbitant degrees.[32] Likewise, efforts could be made to dissuade the Communities from seeking greater self-sufficiency in feed grains and in other sectors where their markets remain relatively open. What should perhaps be more vigorously attacked are the EC's export subsidies and their other questionable competitive practices on third-country markets. International exchanges of information and marketing agreements might help both the United States and the European Communities to anticipate accumulating surpluses in particular commodities and to plan appropriate internal responses before pressures to dump internationally mount. What is also needed is a clearer set of definitions and specifications concerning what kinds of subsidies are internationally illegal under what circumstances, and what forms of retaliation are justifiable in different instances.[33] A case in point concerns U.S. claims that markets for malt in Japan have been undercut by unfair EC competition via subsidies. Here what Washington would like to clarify and codify is that countervailing measures are legitimate where unfair competition on third-country markets takes place. Seeking such clairifications and specifications is a practical goal of American policy.

In an article entitled "Shifting and Sharing Adjustment Burdens: The Role of Industrial Food Importing Nations," Robert Paarlberg argues persuasively that the insulation from the world market accomplished by the CAP may over the longer run redound to the great benefit of the international system.[34] His point is that by moving from high dependency upon imports to near self-sufficiency (and by bearing the high costs of this) the European Communities have reduced total demand for imports and have thereby eliminated a possible source of great strain during times of international shortage. The "crisis" of 1973–74 for example would have been a good deal more severe if Western Europeans laid claim to global food-grain supplies in the way they did 20 years earlier. Rural modernization, including our own, has traditionally been achieved with the aid of tariff protection, and there may be an element of inconsistency in presently encouraging Third World countries to move toward self-sufficiency via modernization, while criticizing Western Europe for accomplishing just that. The external regime of the CAP is likely to be liberalized when the structural reforms of Mansholt's imagination and planning come about, and when the agriculture of the Nine reaches the productive maturity of North America today. Until that time, the United States search for expanded food markets ought to be directed elsewhere, and U.S. support for European governments taking structural reform steps should be included in our economic-policy-coordination efforts.

Preference and Deference
for Less-Developed Countries

Until very recently, Third World countries have not been major participants in the international commercial system, though, as noted, for many of them, food imports have played a crucial and increasing role in meeting their dietary or development objectives. The concerns of the less-developed countries as importers are largely contained in the discussion of price stability above (and more will be said about food security via aid in chapter 3). Fluctuating prices, especially periods of extremely high prices, tend to penalize poorer countries most heavily, and in periods of crisis provoked by short-ages, as in 1973–74, poor countries may be priced entirely out of the market.

Major concerns of LDCs as exporters revolve about their needs to market tropical agricultural products in OECD and some Communist countries in order to raise foreign exchange used either for development or to buy food. Without going into detail with regard to commodity agreements and the debates surrounding them, let it here suffice to say that income stability and steady growth from tropical commodity exports are deemed of utmost importance to Third World countries, and their leaders and advocates quite accurately underline that free market forces guarantee neither. Quite to the contrary, the market, responding to supplies and demands conditioned by myriad factors including weather, can carry tropical exporters through erratic booms and busts. Moreover, many tropical products cannot be stored inexpensively as grain can be. In addition, there is a great deal of empirical evidence to show that the terms of trade with regard to manufactured imports and tropical commodity exports have shifted unfavorably for the latter ever since the 1950s.[35] These factors became the basis for the LDC's case for special treatment on international agricultural markets in the form of commodity agreements. Typical provisions of proposed commodity agreements include stocking schemes, price bands, supply assurances and purchase commitments, plus mechanisms of various sorts to accomplish compensatory financing. Some recent proposals, such as the United Nations Conference on Trade and Development's (UNCTAD) Integrated Commodities Program, also contain provisions for indexing import and export prices facing Third World commodity producers.

The fundamental issue concerning commodity agreements is how well they would serve the goals of their proponents. That is, the principle of special treatment for poor countries is unobjectionable; it is embodied in the General Agreement on Tariffs and Trade (GATT) already. Nor is there anything sacred about the particular form of the "free" market, or anything particularly problematic in moving to a highly regulated regime in some sectors (technical and administrative matters notwithstanding). Nor, again, are stabilization regimes for tropical agricultural products likely to do damage to Western economies. But, on the question of efficacy and benefit to LDCs, the evidence concerning commodity agreements is ambiguous.[36] First, relatively few less-developed countries would actually benefit from the income guarantees of commodity agreements, as relatively few are major commodity exporters. In addition, there is considerable uncertainty among analysts as to exactly how greatly export earnings would be improved as a result of managed buffer stocks. Not all tropical agricultural commodity markets have been characterized by price instability (for example, bananas, cotton, and tea), and some commodities tend to generate reasonably stable export earnings despite price fluctuations (e.g., cocoa, coffee, and sugar). Brazil's coffee stockpiling policies have, of course, contributed to stability in that commodity's market. There is also uncertainty about the income and welfare effects of price stabilization. Second, there is danger that indexing import and export prices would compound world inflation and cancel gains to commodity producers.

In the light of the ambiguity surrounding the issue of commodity agreements, prudence would suggest a positive but cautious stance on the part of the United States and other industrialized countries.[37] An "integrated" commodities program is probably too ambitious in the context of the contemporary international economy, and would certainly be of specific benefit to only some, and likely those who are least in need of support for their export earnings. Careful attention to different countries' dependence upon different commodity exports, and awareness that different formulas are appropriate in different commodity agreements, combined with willingness to accord special treatment to poorer countries on principle, could yield positions on tropical products beneficial to exporters, importers, and the world economy.[38]

One other area of some importance in North-South agricultural relations is the question of access for *processed* agricultural products. Most industrialized countries, including the United States, practice "tariff escalation" by increasing duties on commodities transformed from raw to processed states. Less-developed countries would like to compete in world markets with processed forms of such commodities as fruits, vegetables, meat, fibers, tobacco, and oilseeds, because processing is importantly linked to their industrialization and crucially to higher levels of urban employment. Food processing provides more industrial jobs in Third World countries than any other industry, and providing jobs is perhaps the greatest challenge facing Third World governments in the 1980s. Concessions from industrialized countries on LDC requests for access have been slow and minimal for understandable political and economic reasons (food processing is also a huge industry in our countries!). There is, however, something to be said for more thoroughly thinking through the costs and requirements for adjusting to allow greater access to LDC processed imports. In addition to the potential for trade expansion (for other U.S. products), there are political benefits to our country in abetting industrialization in the Third World and easing unemployment pressures there. These may significantly outweight the costs of dislocation of workers in American food processing industries and should be carefully studied.[39]

Conclusion

The importance of the commercial system as a principal allocator of foodstuffs globally, through direct transfers and indirect economic signals, justifies the extended treatment it receives in this book. Despite the barrage of criticism recently directed against the market, and against those who lead it and profit from it,[40] there is nothing fundamentally awry in the commercial system. It is true that a global concessional system has become needed to complement the commercial system, just as concessional systems function beside commercial ones in market-economy countries to meet the welfare needs of those penalized by free-market allocations. It is also true that markets can abuse their participants, and participants are indeed frequently abused. What this suggests, though, is that no market, including the international food market, should be permitted to function completely without constraints imposed by public policy. Extreme conditions that prevail at the peaks and troughs of market cycles, in particular, can and should be constrained, and the private mercantilistic practices of international grain traders should be controlled. If there is any single overriding obstacle to diplomatically treating the major issues in food marketing today, it lies in the proclivity to cast international debate at the level of economic and political philosophies, well above and beyond specific questions that might otherwise be pragmatically resolved. Often deductive economic logic is substituted for empirical analysis; for instance, in arguing that either a grain reserve should be profitable or it should not exist because it will be "inefficient," a debate we have had with several economic theorists. A world of exploding populations, predictable food deficits, erratically fluctuating prices, and growing dependence upon an imperfect market is hardly served by philosophic debate in lieu of action.

CHAPTER 3

The Concessional System: From Dumping to Development

Historical Background

American food aid was institutionalized in 1954 with the passage of Public Law 480, the Agricultural Trade Development and Assistance Act. This legislation wedded two American traditions of international food transfers: emergency or disaster relief and surplus disposal. The first tradition, large-scale emergency food relief, occurred particularly in the aftermaths of World War I and World War II. The United States, at those times provided substantial grain, principally to Europe, to stave off widespread food shortages and prospective famine. These were probably the most substantial instances of gifts of food to attack emergency situations in world history. The second tradition that prepared the way for the formal American food-aid program was the practice of surplus disposal. Following the farm-support legislation passed during the depression of the early 1930s, the Grain Stabilization Board (GSB) and the Commodity Credit Corporation (CCC) were established. Whereas previous foreign sales were basically in private hands, the GSB was empowered to make sales to foreign governments, to give price concessions, and even to provide gifts.[1] As the CCC began to purchase and hold inventories of surplus crops in order to fulfill its mandate to prevent prices of individual commodities from falling below targeted minimum prices, pressure to dispose of inventories grew. In order to dispose of these according to terms of the international wheat agreement as signed in 1949, the United States was pledged to an effort not to disrupt commercial markets through dumping its surplus at cheap prices.[2] In this context, then, it is not surprising to find instances in which the surplus-disposal managers in the Department of Agriculture were pressed by potential "buyers" to sweeten deals. While surpluses were lowered briefly by the Korean War, by 1953, government officials in Colombia were able to offer to take "cheap grain" from the United States provided the United States would also provide additional foreign assistance.[3]

A further impetus to the institutionalization of concessional food sales was the Marshall Plan. This massive program of aid, along with other foreign assistance efforts that developed in the late 1940s with the onset of the Cold War, established a precedent for long-term regular American foreign assistance. In 1948–49, for instance, 60 percent of United States agricultural exports were financed by foreign aid programs.[4]

Beginning in 1954, following the passage of the PL480 act, a more systematic and coordinated program of concessional food sales, barters, and food donations was inaugurated, and it was done under the aegis of the Department of Agriculture. In particular, the Foreign Agricultural Service (FAS), with its proximity as a part of the Agriculture Department to the operation of domestic programs whose surpluses were to be exported, understandably became the agency to administer the PL480 program. Moreover, Agriculture had just regained control of the agricultural attaché service and incorporated it into FAS. From the 1930s until 1951, overseas attachés had been under the direction of the Department of State, as had the aid programs that paid for overseas food disposal after World War II. However, when the food aid program was legislated in 1954, powerful farm interests in the agriculture committees of Congress and in the Department of Agriculture blocked significant involvement of the foreign-affairs community in setting up the new food aid program.

Since its inauguration, the food aid program has undergone

Table 3.1 U.S. Agricultural Exports: Concessional Government-Financed Programs and Total, Value and Percent of Total, Fiscal Years 1955-1976, July–September 1976 and October–September 1977-1978

Year	Public Law 480						Mutual Security AID[f]	Total Agricultural Exports		
	Sales for local currency[a]	Long-term dollar and convertible local currency credit sales[b]	Government-to-government donations and World Food Program[c]	Donation through voluntary relief agencies[d]	Barter for strategic materials[e]	Total P.L. 480		Under specified Government programs	Outside specified Government programs[g]	Total[h]
	$ Million									
1955	73	—	52	135	125	385	450	835	2,309	3,144
1956	439	—	63	184	298	984	355	1,339	2,157	3,496
1957	908	—	51	165	401	1,525	394	1,919	2,809	4,728
1958	657	—	51	173	100	981	227	1,208	2,795	4,003
1959	724	—	30	131	132	1,017	210	1,227	2,492	3,719
1960	824	—	38	105	149	1,116	167	1,283	3,236	4,519
1961	951	—	75	146	144	1,316	186	1,502	3,444	4,946
1962	1,030	19	88	160	198	1,495	74	1,569	3,573	5,142
1963	1,088	57	89	174	48	1,456	14	1,470	3,608	5,078
1964	1,056	48	81	189	43	1,417	24	1,441	4,627	6,068
1965	1,142	158	55	183	32	1,570	26	1,596	4,501	6,097
1966	866	181	87	180	32	1,346	42	1,388	5,359	6,747
1967	803	178	110	157	23	1,271	37	1,308	5,513	6,821
1968	723	300	100	150	6	1,279	18	1,297	5,086	6,383
1969	346	427	111	154	1	1,039	11	1,050	4,776	5,826
1970	309	506	113	128	—	1,056	12	1,068	5,650	6,718
1971	204	539	138	142	—	1,023	56	1,079	6,674	7,753
1972	143	535	228	152	—	1,058	66	1,124	6,922	8,046
1973	6	661	159	128	—	954	84	1,038	11,864	12,902
1974	-	575	147	145	—	867	76	943	20,350	21,293
1975	—	762	148	191	—	1,101	123	1,224	20,354	21,578
1976	—	650	65	192	—	907	216	1,123	21,024	22,147
July–Sept. 1976	—	316	18	51	—	385	138	523	4,832	5,355
Oct.–Sept. 1976/77	—	760	92	250	—	1,102	419	1,521	22,453	23,974
Oct.–Sept. 1977/78	—	730	112	204			477	1,514		

74

Year									
1956	13	—	2	5	8	28	10	38	62	100
1957	19	—	1	4	9	33	8	41	59	100
1958	16	—	1	4	3	24	6	30	70	100
1959	19	—	1	3	4	27	6	33	67	100
1960	18	—	1	2	3	24	4	28	72	100
1961	19	—	—	3	3	26	4	30	70	100
1962	20	—	2	3	4	29	1	30	70	100
1963	22	1	2	3	1	29	—	29	71	100
1964	17	1	1	3	1	23	1	24	76	100
1965	19	3	1	3	—	26	—	26	74	100
1966	13	3	1	3	—	20	1	21	79	100
1967	12	3	2	2	—	19	—	19	81	100
1968	11	5	2	2	—	20	—	20	80	100
1969	6	7	2	3	—	18	—	18	82	100
1970	5	7	2	2	—	16	—	16	84	100
1971	2	7	2	2	—	13	1	14	86	100
1972	2	6	3	2	—	13	1	14	86	100
1973	—	5	1	1	—	7	1	8	92	100
1974	—	2	1	1	—	4	—	4	96	100
1975	—	3	1	—	—	5	1	6	94	100
1976	—	3	1	1	—	4	1	5	95	100
July–Sept. 1976	—	6	1	1	—	7	3	10	90	100
Oct.–Sept. 1976/77	—	3	1	1	—	4	2	6	94	100
Oct.–Sept. 1977/78	—	3	1	1	—	4	2	6	94	100
1955 through Oct.–Sept. 1978	5	3	2	2	1	12	2	14	86	100

SOURCE: *Foreign Agricultural Trade of the United States* (Washington, D.C.: U.S. Dept. of Agriculture, January, 1979), p. 57.

NOTE: October–September 1976/77 is the beginning of the new fiscal year. No comparison is made for the October–September 1975/76 year.

— = Not applicable.

[a]Authorized by Title I, P.L. 480. [b]Shipments under agreements signed through Dec. 31, 1966, authorized by Title IV, P.L. 480. Shipments under agreements signed from Jan. 1, 1967, authorized by Title I, P.L. 480, as amended by P.L. 89-808. [c]Authorized by Title II, P.L. 480. Includes World Food Program. [d]Authorized by Section 416 of the Agricultural Act of 1949 and Section 302, Title III, P.L. 480 through Dec. 31, 1966. Authorized by Title II, P.L. 480, as amended by P.L. 89-808, effective Jan. 1, 1949. [e]Authorized by Section 303, Title III, P.L. 480, and other legislation. Includes some shipments in exchange for goods and services for U.S. agencies before 1963. [f]Sales for foreign currency, economic aid, and expenditures under development loans authorized by P.L.'s 165, 665, and 87-195. [g]"Total agricultural exports outside specified Government programs" (sales for dollars) include in addition to unassisted commercial transactions, shipments of some commodities with governmental assistance in the form of (1) barter shipments for overseas procurement for U.S. agencies; (2) extension of credit guarantees for relatively short periods; (3) sales of Government-owned commodities at less than domestic market prices, and (4) export payments in case or in kind. [h]Data does not include furskins, bulk tobacco, citric acid, fatty acids, glues, and adhesives n.e.c., 1966–71. [i]Less than $500,000. [j]Less than .5 percent.

75

Table 3.2 Food Aid in Cereals[a] by Principal Donors
(in thousand tons)

	1971/72	1972/73	1973/74	1974/75	1975/76	1976/77	1977/78	1978/79
Argentina	13	2	10	20	—	22	34	23[b]
Australia	215	259	222	330	261	231	252	314
Canada	1,093	887	486	594	1,034	1,176	1,000	1,000
EEC	978	986	1,208	1,413	928	1,131	1,451	1,287[b]
Finland	—	25	17	24	25	33	47	14[b]
Japan	731	528	350	182	33	46	141	225[b]
Norway	8	—	—	—	10	10	10	10
Sweden	8	56	65	316	47	122	105	75
Switzerland	27	21	33	29	35	33	22	32[b]
United States[c]	9,259	7,025	3,198	4,712	4,284	6,147	5,896	6,162[d]
Others[e]	231	320	62	753[f]	199	137	395	400
Total	12,563	10,109	5,651[g]	8,373	6,856	9,088	9,353	9,542

SOURCE: *Food Outlook* (Rome: Food and Agriculture Organization, no. 1979)

[a] For the period 1971/72 to 1977/78 figures relate to shipments during July/June. For 1978/79 figures relate to allocations for the budgetary period of each country concerned, except when otherwise indicated.
[b] FAC commitments for the July/June period.
[c] Includes wheat and coarse grains products and blended foods in grain equivalent.
[d] Indicative planning figure as of January 1979. Title III included.
[e] Includes occasional food aid from various donors on a calendar year basis.
[f] Includes food aid provided through UNEO in 1974/75.
[g] In addition the USSR made wheat loans of 2 million tons to India and 200,000 tons to Bangladesh, both repayable in kind.

substantial modification. Amendments to the legislation in 1959 and 1966 increased its utility in assisting United States balance of payments, while amendments in 1966, 1975, and 1977 increased the humanitarian and developmental thrust of the program and placed limits on its use as a mechanism of adjustment for domestic farm policy.

Another important change in the global concessional system has been the growth of food aid programs by other countries, spawned in part by the American model and formally encouraged by the United States, most openly through the Food Aid Convention (FAC), initially drawn up as a companion to the International Wheat Agreement when it was renewed in 1967. During the late 1950s and early 1960s, American food aid was at its zenith in size. It accounted for over 30 percent of all American agricultural exports, constituted over 90 percent of total international food assistance, and in absolute terms regularly amounted to as much as 15 to 17 million metric tons of grain annually, about three times the annual average since 1973. In the period 1974–77, concessional transfers accounted for 4 percent to 7 percent of total American food exports (down from 20 percent to 40 percent) and represented only about 60 percent of the total flow of food assistance. (See tables 3.1 and 3.2.) Canada and the European Community were the other major donors in this period. In spite of this downward trend, the American food assistance program remains the largest and the most complex element in overall concessional food flows in the world. The United States continues to be the leader both in supplying food and providing management for the global system of concessional international food transfers.

Goal Served By Food Aid

Food aid serves both domestic and foreign policy goals. Although the program has come to have increasing importance for the international purposes it serves, its value as an instrument to serve domestic farm and economic policy remains an important basis for its support in Congress, in the government bureaucracy, among select producer and industry groups, and in the public. Indeed, a coalition of international and humanitarian interests, represented by church groups and development-oriented citizen bodies, such as the Foreign Policy Association and the Overseas Development Council, combines with support from major farm and commodity organizations, trading firms, and some of the major processors to make food aid a unique component in the total flow of overseas development assistance. Few, if any, other aid programs have the substantial backing of domestic interests enjoyed by food aid. This greater base of political support, however, is also a source of tension; the use of food aid as a component in overseas development assistance rests less on its effectiveness in promoting foreign policy goals, such as the economic development and welfare of recipient countries, and more on its role in satisfying domestic policy goals. In the best cases of food aid, multiple goals or objectives will be served simultaneously, thus allowing supporters of the program to construe the same action as serving the particular interests they seek to promote, even though these interests are quite diverse. The congressional coalitions that have supported food aid programs are politically heterogeneous. People with very different perspectives of the world, and of the values food aid should serve, have united in a common cause, at least as long as the program as a whole has served each of their goals, albeit diverse. This blending of interests can be particularly happy for legislators who see themselves as promoting international philanthropic goals and represent a farm constituency as, for example, Senator Hubert Humphrey did. His interest in, and support of, food aid led to a happy merging of these broad interests and his efforts from major hearings in 1958 onward consistently broadened the scope and deepened the institutionalization of the program.

Food aid serves two basic goals for domestic policy—the disposal (hopefully benign) of surplus farm commodities and the development of overseas commercial markets. A third domestic goal, controlling inflation, is also important from time to time. During the 1950s and 1960s, when the inventories of the Commodity Credit Corporation were substantial, the two principal domestic objectives alone provided adequate justification for the program. Domestic support for the program was seen as so strong by some recipients that on occasion one or another made an effort to secure additional "benefits" from the United States in return for helping the United States get rid of unwanted surpluses. It also created confidence among recipients that America would meet their needs. This is reflected in the response of an Indian government official to a question (by Secretary of Agriculture Orville Freeman during a visit in 1961) about what reserves India had as insurance against a bad crop year. He replied; "Oh, they're in Kansas."[5]

Food aid to such countries as Japan, Korea, Mexico, and Iran are good illustrations of the role food aid can play in helping develop overseas markets. In Korea, for example, since 1955, approximately 38 percent of all Korean agricultural imports from the United States have been financed under PL480 or direct AID programs. In fiscal 1976, however, Korea imported $772 million in agricultural products of which $63 million, or less than 9 percent, arrived under long-term sales on the PL480 concessional terms. Japan in the 1950s received over $300 million in PL480 aid, mostly for local currency; by 1976, Japan imported over $3.3 billion in agricultural goods from the United States, all through the commercial system.

The pressure to push commodities heavily inventoried by the CCC through PL480 sales is a strong characteristic of the system which has never been completely absent. Rules to minimize conflicts among exporting countries over price cutting emerged both formally and informally in the 1950s and helped legitimize and institutionalize food aid in the international system. Canadians, for example, were relatively tolerant of use of PL480 in Europe and Japan, as long as the Cold War climate prevented the U.S. from competing in Eastern

European markets. During the 1950s Canada regularly sold grain to Eastern Europe, the Soviet Union, and China. The surplus disposal committee set up under the Food and Agricultural Organization became another vehicle for working out protests over sales which might allegedly cut out other countries from commercial sales. Indeed, limitations of PL480 agreements prohibit a recipient country from exporting within one year the same kind of commodities. Also legislation requires American officials to claim that PL480 sales are in excess and not in place of commercial sales. Such rules have tended to limit the extent to which PL480 could be used to dump surpluses or unambiguously disrupt the commercial markets. While all partici-pants believe that PL480 shipments have in fact substituted in some cases and to some extent for commercial sales, few blatant cases of market "stealing" have ocurred. Moreover, it has been hard to detect to what extent commerical markets were being undercut. In any event, by 1962, following the establishment of the World Food Pro-gram, and reinforced in 1967 by the Food Aid Convention, the practice of giving away or selling food on terms substantially below that of the current market became an accepted international practice, albeit at that time almost completely dominated by the United States.

The pervasiveness of the surplus-disposal motivation in the 1970s can be seen even during the period of food crisis, 1973–74, when pressure to have the United States export rice—still in surplus in the U.S.—continued, despite its less helpful value to desperate recipients compared to the relatively less expensive wheat or feed-grain crops. In the spring of 1978, Canadians were disturbed to find that the United States had sold to Mexico large quantities of nonfat dry milk, which, in their opinion, undercut potential established and expected Canadian sales to Mexico. And Canadians baulked at proposed PL480 wheat to Haiti in 1978, because it threatened their commercial wheat exports—indeed, wheat to be made into flour in a Haitian mill financed by the Canadians. Thus, the United States continues to use food aid as a surplus-disposal mechanism; but it does so substantially

Table 3.3 Major Recipients of PL480 Aid, Title I, Title II, and Total, Fiscal Years 1955-76[a]
(*in $ million*)

Country	1955-64	1965-74	1975-76	1955-76 Title I	1955-76 Title II	Total[b]
India	2,084	2,933	301	4,406	836	5,318
Pakistan	736	906	175	1,688	129	1,817
South Korea	493	1,034	128	1,339	310	1,655
South Vietnam	130	1,307	27	1,308	156	1,464
Egypt	690	222	220	976	143	1,132
Indonesia	212	757	56	940	83	1,025
Yugoslavia	783	238	—	848	153	1,021
Brazil	501	385	7	607	224	893
Israel	289	375	24	621	21	688
Turkey	452	218	4	550	106	674
Spain	604	18	—	474	117	622
Poland	535	33	—	498	60	568
Bangladesh	—	66	364	378	52	430
Italy	403	3	—	140	232	406
Republic of China	237	158	—	293	86	395
Morocco	97	264	24	155	226	385
United Kingdom	342	11	—	48	—	353
Chile	128	112	110	238	107	350
Tunisia	96	200	12	166	141	308
Khmer Republic	—	207	91	295	3	298
Philippines	89	167	25	134	132	281
Colombia	118	131	18	110	142	267
Greece	202	43	—	144	88	245
West Germany	212	3	—	1	66	215
World total	11,692	11,463	1,932	17,853	5,502	25,087

SOURCES: *1974 Annual Report on Public Law 480;* Foreign Agricultural Trade of the United States, Oct. 1976; 12 Years of Achievement under Public Law 480, Economic Research Service Foreign Report No. 202 1967; and *U.S. Agricultural Exports under Public Law 480, 1974,* ERS Foreign Report No. 395; *Foreign Agricultural Trade,* U.S. Dept. of Agriculture, July 1978, p. 34.

[a]Includes all countries which directly received over $200 million under all titles of P.L. 480—sales, grants, and barter—during fiscal years 1955-76.
[b]The residual between the total and the sum of Titles I (local currency, dollar credit and convertible local currency credit sales) and II (grants and donations) is Title III (barter).

Table 3.4 U.S. Agricultural Exports:
Specified Government-Financed Programs, Calendar Year 1977

| | Public Law 480 | | | | | |
| | Title I Credit Sales[a] | Government-Government | Title II donations[b] | | | |
Country			Voluntary Relief Agencies	World Food Program	AID	Total Government
			1,000 dollars			
All commodities:	706,329	36,560	249,504	81,657	419,260	1,493,311
Guatemala	—	—	5,685	101	—	5,786
El Salvador	—	—	1,369	1,037	—	2,406
Honduras	—	—	2,619	506	—	3,125
Nicaragua	—	—	—	354	—	352
Costa Rica	—	—	2,946	276	—	3,221
Panama	—	—	1,804	—	—	1,804
Jamaica	5,340	—	—	4	—	5,344
Haiti	11,067	—	8,502	1,064	—	20,633
Dominican Republic	—	—	7,905	—	—	7,905
Barbados	—	—	—	161	—	161
Colombia	—	—	3,574	1,037	—	4,611
Guyana	—	—	—	7	—	7
Ecuador	—	—	750	824	—	1,574
Peru	—	549	2,575	2,199	—	5,321
Bolivia	—	61	6,160	618	—	6,839
Chile	—	—	16,990	—	—	16,990
Brazil	—	—	—	1,017	—	1,017
Paraguay	—	—	—	180	—	180
Portugal	68,231	—	—	—	—	68,231
Romania	—	413	—	—	—	413
Turkey						815

Israel	1,722	—	1,176	—	281,881	284,779
Jordan	9,691	—	103	1,907	—	11,701
Gaza strip	—	—	1,076	—	—	1,076
Yemen (Sana)	—	—	367	170	—	536
Afghanistan	—	—	—	818	—	818
India	25,994	—	85,270	5,817	—	117,031
Pakistan	36,924	—	256	321	—	37,502
Nepal	—	—	—	1,554	—	1,554
Bangladesh	59,519	—	9,824	16,414	—	85,757
Sri Lanka (Ceylon)	36,288	—	4,149	415	—	40,852
Indonesia	87,269	—	3,748	4,369	—	95,406
Philippines	13,171	12,718	23,039	113	—	49,041
Southern Asia, NEC	—	—	—	73	—	73
Korea, Republic of	77,756	—	—	—	—	77,756
Bhutan	—	—	—	73	—	73
Morocco	9,593	—	15,627	—	—	25,220
Algeria	—	—	—	8,328	—	8,328
Tunisia	8,652	—	5,491	508	—	14,652
Egypt	194,371	—	6,221	5,183	137,379	343,154
Sudan	4,764	—	289	1,993	—	7,025
Mauritania	—	—	110	1,225	—	1,335
Cameroon	—	—	778	125	—	903
Senegal	—	552	3,425	877	—	4,854
Mali	—	—	—	297	—	297
Guinea	3,041	—	—	160	—	3,201
Sierra Leone	1,294	—	621	23	—	1,938
Ivory Coast	—	—	—	153	—	153
Ghana	—	1,055	3,427	609	—	5,091
The Gambia	—	296	712	416	—	837
Niger	—	—	—	219	—	219
Togo	—	735	797	1,267	—	2,799
Central African Republic	—	—	—	68	—	68

Table 3.4 (Continued)

Country	Title I Credit Sales[a]	Public Law 480 — Title II donations[b] Government-Government	Voluntary Relief Agencies	World Food Program	AID	Total Government
Chad	—	2,630	934	1,363	—	4,926
Upper Volta	—	1,543	6,108	537	—	8,189
Dahomey (Benin)	—	—	163	509	—	690
Western Africa, N.E.C.	—	2,632	—	333	—	2,965
Congo (Brazzaville)	—	—	—	724	—	724
Liberia	—	—	—	60	—	60
Zaire	18,463	—	—	—	—	18,463
Burundi	—	—	773	570	—	1,344
Rwanda	—	276	1,214	132	—	1,622
Somali Republic	—	—	—	88	—	88
Ethiopia	—	410	1,967	1,672	—	4,148
Kenya	—	—	1,148	—	—	1,148
Seychelles	—	—	147	—	—	147
Tanzania	7,594	4,581	3,389	—	—	15,564
Mauritius	—	—	—	433	—	433
Mozambique	—	4,405	—	—	—	4,405
Malagasy Republic	—	—	1,171	32	—	1,203
Botswana	—	—	—	2,180	—	2,180
Zambia	4,582	—	—	33	—	4,615
Swaziland	—	—	—	104	—	104
Malawi	—	—	—	176	—	176
Lesotho	—	—	2,571	1,406	—	3,977

SOURCE: Foreign Agricultural Trade, U.S. Department of Agriculture, June 1978, p. 28.

less heavily than does Europe, with its powdered milk aid, and it remains an element in the program of far less importance than a decade or two earlier.[6] Indeed, a review of table 3.3, which lists the major recipients of PL480 over the years, reveals a marked contrast with the list of all recipients in 1977 given in table 3.4. This contrast indicates the shift in priorities among goals, as well as shifts in the needs of key recipients, except for Egypt and India, in recent years.

While surplus disposal and market development are closely related to domestic American farm programs aimed at finding markets or uses for American agricultural surpluses (generated because of efforts designed to increase farm income), such efforts can be too successful. In this case, another domestic objective, holding down inflation, comes into play. Since 1972, the Council of Economic Advisers and the Treasury Department have been especially concerned about the effect of tight supplies on the American economy quite generally. Macroeconomic policy, experts now argue, must be served not only by preventing a depression in the farm sector, but also by preventing excessive price rises in food from fueling inflation throughout the economy. Indeed, inflation generated by rises in food prices will affect not only the United States but every important food importing country as well. In April, 1973, precisely such inflationary fears led to a halt in all PL480 commitments and the establishment of an ad hoc committee chaired by the Office of Management and Budget to review the supply situation in order to determine what level of food aid could be tolerated in light of the rapidly rising prices in the United States. The dramatic drop in U.S. food aid tonnage in 1973–74 is attributable both to the fact that with rising costs the same dollar amount programmed for food aid could buy and ship fewer quantities of commodities, and to the fact that the dollar amount was cut back in light of the inflationary pressure which every foreign sale had on the American grain markets.[7] Because of the tightness of food aid in the "crisis" period compared to a decade earlier, food-deficit countries had to increase their commercial imports markedly. India and Bangladesh, for instance, purchased substantial amounts of grain in the commercial markets in order to maintain adequate food supplies, at least in their urban areas (see figure 1.1). As noted earlier, the objectives of the PL480 program came into sharpest conflict with each other and with the patterns of expectations of recipient countries during this period of shortage.

It may be argued that if domestic goals had been overriding during the crisis period, food aid programs would have been cut out entirely, yet at least three nonhumanitarian considerations assured minimal food aid flows in spite of their possible effect of increasing American inflation.[8] First there was substantial pressure from those with stakes in the maintenance of minimal continuity in the program for its domestic value. This included producers, for whom food inflation is not entirely undesirable, and processors and bureaucratic government and private charitable agencies with a stake in maintaining their programs and areas of access, whether for market development and surplus disposal or for the goods and services they provide. For them, it was important to keep the policy instrument for doing this intact. A second consideration was the political and economic importance to American overseas interests in having food aid as a policy tool. This is exemplified in the quick offer of food aid to Chile in 1973 following Allende's overthrow—a reward for those likely to side with U.S. political and economic interests. In general then, foreign policy considerations, including a desire to influence others through inducements—as well as a concern for economic development—helped sustain the program. Yet a third consideration was the legal commitment of the United States under the Food Aid Conventions (FAC) to supply a minimum of 1.9 million tons of grain or about 45 percent of the total grain committed under this international agreement. If the United States defaulted on its minimum obligations, other countries, upon which the United States had been pressing to bear a greater share of the burden of adjustment for shortage-induced high prices, might also default, thereby driving international prices even higher. International price rises affected the United States more heavily than they did, for instance, the European Community, whose food aid minimum pledge was about two-thirds that of the United States.

Overall, six overseas goals for food aid can be identified. These often combine in justifying food aid to a particular country, but more often than not one or another can be seen to be especially important in a particular case. The six considerations are: (1) financial concerns, such as balance of payments problems or protection of foreign investments; (2) promotion of the economic development of the recipient country; (3) emergency relief; (4) nutritional deficiencies; (5) political objectives such as promoting friendship and providing support to particular governments and their leaders; and (6) specific quid pro quo political deals in which food aid is exchanged for some reciprocal action.

Food aid to Jamaica illustrates well the role that international financial considerations have played in aid policy. Initially, Jamaica received a considerable portion of food aid under Title II (full grant aid). Over time, however, Jamaica was shifted to Title I, or concessional sales, where perhaps only 60 percent to 75 percent of the total value of the food shipped under PL480 could be considered a grant or concession. In 1974, when Jamaica abruptly raised prices of bauxite exports to the United States and fear rose that American aluminum investments might be expropriated, all PL480 programs were suspended. The rationale for the suspension was both political—a warning to the Jamaicans about retaliation for economic "warfare"—and economic, forcing the Jamaicans in essence to pay higher prices for food imports. Whether Jamaican imports came from the United States or not, the effect would be beneficial to the American balance of payments.

Economic development objectives may be seen in food aid flows to Indonesia or the Philippines. Food that flows under World Food Program auspices and/or goes to support "food-for-work" projects is particularly thought to have development as a principle objective. Economic development, of course, can be fostered through a variety of final uses, depending on the context. Food aid that serves as general balance-of-payments assistance, if it frees foreign exchange for use in development projects, can be considered developmental.[9]

The third category, emergency relief, is exemplified in emergency shipments to the Sahelian countries in West Africa and Ethiopia during the drought periods in the early 1970s; and to Guatemala, following the disastrous earthquake in 1975. Such "emergency" relief usually amounts to a small proportion of the total flow of food aid. While emergencies arise with some regularity, they are acute rather than chronic needs. American food in these cases almost always comes from the Title II category, in the form of grants to agencies that deliver food to disaster areas. Occasionally such assistance may not be appropriate, as in Guatemala, where it apparently depressed prices of grain from the local harvest which was not affected by the earthquake.

Title II grants are also given for nutritional purposes. This fourth international objective has been given increased prominence in American legislation and rhetoric. School feeding programs, mother-child health centers and rural food for work programs have all been set up by American voluntary agencies, notably CARE and Catholic Relief Services, with a principal aim of getting food to the most undernourished and nutritionally vulnerable portions of populations in a wide variety of poor countries. From Burundi to Yemen, small scale feeding programs spread thinly the largesse of American food abundance to the chronically disadvantaged. Few such efforts are large in scale, reflecting the modest priority of nutrition objectives.

Political objectives, in contrast, tend to be basic and pervasive. When Henry Kissinger visited Egypt in the winter of 1973–74, American food assistance to Egypt had not been in effect for nearly six years, having ceased after the break in relations following the 1967

Arab-Israeli war. Kissinger cabled Washington during his visit to Cairo, proposing substantial amounts of grain be sent to Egypt. He and State Department officials were hoping food aid could offer Egypt concrete evidence of American goodwill during a period in which most food aid recipients had been cut back from previous supply levels. An initial commitment of grain plus additional amounts during 1974 were provided to Egypt. Such aid came at a time when Egypt was particularly hard-pressed to meet its domestic food needs and had to spend substantial amounts of its scarce foreign exchange for food imports. In return for American aid, the Egyptians were expected to reopen diplomatic relations with the United States and to work toward disengagement with Israel and a solution to Middle East conflict, based on American rather than Soviet resources and good offices. Since then, food aid to Egypt has increased to become the largest sent to any country. Although political friendship is certainly the key consideration to explain the episodic ebbs and flows in American food aid to Egypt (see figure 3.1), there are genuine and substantial economic development and humanitarian-nutritional concerns that have also been served. Similarly the flow to Israel has been substantial and rose in tandem with Egypt after 1974. However, because of the 1975 legislation limiting no more than 25 percent of Title I concessional sales to countries other than "poor" ones (in 1979, these are countries eligible for World Bank (IDA) loans because of their low per capita GNP), Israel's food imports under PL480 have ended. However, the Commodity Import Program of AID which goes to countries receiving military support (or Security Supporting Assistance) now pays for a large portion of Israel's food imports. In fiscal 1978, this amounted to $243 million for Israel and $232 million for Egypt. Thus $475 million in AID balance-of-payment support outside of PL480 was a form of food aid divorced from domestic supply considerations and allocated almost entirely for political purposes.

Egypt since 1974 is a good case showing how food aid may serve

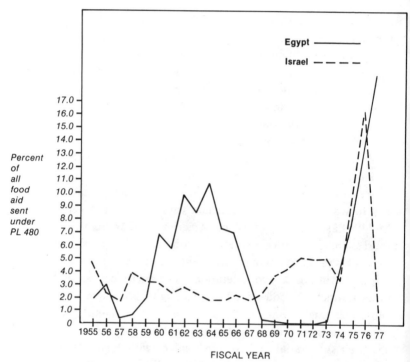

Figure 3.1
The Percent of Food Assistance to Egypt and Israel, 1955–76

a mix of foreign-policy goals simultaneously. By 1976, serious concerns were raised about the impact of food assistance on Egypt's
economy and the income of peasant farmers. One result of this
concern led the United States and the International Monetary Fund
to pressure the Egyptian government to raise the price of food in
urban areas. This would force consumers to recognize a price closer
to the "realistic" one that had to be paid for food, and would encourage farmers to expand their output to receive higher prices. However,
when riots ensued in Cairo, Sadat's government seemed threatened.
To restore stability and possibly prevent the toppling of Sadat, the
United States quickly reversed its policy and extended additional

food supplies under PL480 and Security Supporting Assistance Programs. Political considerations, therefore, remain the prominent factor in supplying food aid to Egypt.

The other way in which food aid has been used to pursue foreign-policy objectives, one not directly tied to balance of payments, economic development, or nutritional well being, occurs when food aid has been tied to the specific *quid pro quo* requests of the American administration or Congress. In 1966 and 1967, for instance, Lyndon Johnson tried to extract concessions from India in return for the large grain shipments sent there to relieve near-famine conditions. More recently minor *quid pro quo's* have been extracted from countries on human rights issues (an embargo on aid was put on for doubtful countries in the fall of 1977) or with respect to features of their trade elsewhere (as in the demand that Bangladesh stop exporting jute to Cuba). Furthermore, in June 1978, the House of Representatives threatened to sever $50 million of scheduled food assistance for South Korea until the Korean government provided their former Ambassador to the United States to the House subcommittee investigating charges of bribery to congressmen by Koreans in the early 1970s. After the House voted an amendment, the threat was successful and Senate action was not needed.

Beyond the frequently used political supports provided by food aid, as in the case of Vietnam and Cambodia in the early 1970s and Chile and Israel more recently, *quid pro quo's* related to agricultural development have become more common. This is apparent first with the "self-help" requirements of Title I begun in 1966, where it was made mandatory that recipient countries enumerate specific steps they were taking to improve self-sufficiency in food production. Since 1977, a new program, Title III, the so-called "Food for Development" section of the new agricultural and foreign-assistance legislation, has been designed to provide recipient countries with greater incentives to use food as a developmental tool. While the first Title III agreements (with Bolivia, Bangladesh and Egypt) were not concluded until 1978 or later, American experience in discussing such agreements, as with Indonesia, Pakistan, and Zaire, suggests that tough conditions can be proposed requiring recipient countries to improve the progressive quality of their agriculture and rural-development policies.

The fact remains that of the nine objectives, three domestic and six foreign, which have been enumerated above, at least four or five and in some cases all nine might seem to be present in any particular food aid flow, especially bilateral ones. Multilateral food aid channels tend to be less useful as means for specifically satisfying American domestic-policy objectives or foreign political objectives. This may explain in part why the U.S. commitments to the World Food Program have declined in recent years, from 35 percent in 1969–70 to 26 percent in 1977–78 of the Program's resources and from 18.4 percent of Title II allocations in 1976 to 15 percent in 1979. Multilateral channels are more prone to emphasize humanitarian, developmental, and emergency-relief objectives. The resolution on food aid supported at the World Food Conference by the United States has called for increasing aid commitments from one to three years, and for increasing the amount sent in multilateral channels. These objectives, agreed upon at the Conference, have been followed very little in practice by the United States. At a minimum, the United States has moved to make an increasing proportion of its food aid under Title III availiable on a longer-term basis (usually three years), and has announced a provisional new minimum pledge for a FAC of 4.5 million metric tons of grain (up from 1.9). Many uncertainties remain, however, about the future directions of the food aid program in the United States. Important unresolved questions concern, first, whether American programs will in fact become more multilateral and multi-year in their orientation, and second, whether food aid will return to the high quantity levels of a decade ago or instead be slowly phased out as commercial sales (now over 90 percent of agricultural exports) and direct financial assistance replace concessional commodity shipments.

Issue of Food Aid

At least five important questions can be raised about the food aid program of the United States. These questions entail a series of particular aguments and perspectives relating to the purpose and consequences of food aid. We shall briefly sketch out the issues raised by each of these five questions and indicate the resolution that we find most attractive. The five questions are:

1. How permanent should food aid be?

2. What priorities should be given to the various goals that food aid serves?

3. If economic development and agricultural modernization are prime goals, can food aid really support them?

4. What governmental organization would be most effective for implementing the program (as worked out in answer to the above questions)?

5. What should be the relationship between American food aid programs and policies and those of other governments and international organizations?

Permanency of Food Aid

Exasperation or cynicism has led various observers of American Food Aid policy to suggest that it might be well to eliminate the program. Emma Rothchild, for example, has proposed that the program has more detrimental effects than positive ones and that it should be consciously phased out over the next decade.[10] Arthur Mead, until recently sales manager for the PL480 program in the Department of Agriculture, suggested out of exasperation in 1975 that the Department of Agriculture would be just as happy to get rid of the Food Aid program.[11] Mead's statement is not representative of the current Department of Agriculture, nor his own reasoned position, but it did reflect accurately the frustrations felt by many in the department at a time when Congress was passing legislation to impose more stringent constraints on the direction of such aid and the eligibility of recipients. At the same time, American surpluses had dwindled to a point where the domestic objectives of food aid were no longer salient.

A somewhat different position from that of those who would advocate or acquiesce in terminating the Food Aid program, is that taken by those who argue that "self-liquidating food aid" should be pursued vis-a-vis each chronic recipient. This perspective, shared by many who are eager to see development go forward, would emphasize the use of food aid only in ways that eventually eliminated its need. The point is to make food aid compatible with the goal that each country should be physically or at least economically self-reliant with respect to its food supply, a goal widely articulated and seemingly unchallengeable as a benign objective. Indeed, if recipient countries were required to take concrete, plausible steps toward agricultural and general economic development as a condition for food aid, their prospects for overcoming their reliance on concessional imports should improve. This would entail, however, substantial changes in the way in which food aid is administered by both donors and recipients. Moreover, substantial projected deficits for food-poor countries, cited in chapter 1, suggest that it is unreasonable to imagine the need for food aid diminishing over the next decade. In fact, FAO estimates are that food-aid minimum needs will grow from 10 million tons to 16 million tons by 1985. Even concerted and energetic effort on the part of chronic food-aid recipients may be inadequate to raise their productivity to a point where they could enjoy both self-sustaining economic growth and meet their food needs from domestic production or commercial imports. With continuing population growth over the next decade or two, countries such as Bangladesh, Egypt, and many others are likely to continue to find food aid a desirable and necessary ingredient in their overall economic situation.

A third position is to imagine the indefinite continuation of food aid as a component of overseas development assistance, as well as for emergency relief situations. Such a reaffirmation of food aid also assumes that some of the major criticisms of past food aid policies can be overcome. This position does not reject the notion of self-liquidation, but rather argues that to build sunset provisions or other tough requirements into food aid might dangerously reduce flexibility to meet development needs over the next decade, and might more easily fail in any event if the desired elimination of need were not realized. This third position, therefore, seems the most realistic to us.

It is unrealistic to plan for a general phasing out of food aid or even individual phasing out for specific countries for several reasons. To accomplish this without a loss to American influence abroad would require substantially changed perspectives among recipients. Since the mid-1960s there has been renewed interest within developing countries in promoting agricultural modernization and rural development with food aid as a means of assisting. Since urban and industrial projects, along with social-overhead infrastructure, absorbed the largest portion of most developing countries' investment resources, efforts to use food aid as a developmental resource have been widely promoted. Further, the assumption, as made by Rothchild and others, that an equivalent amount of cash aid could be substituted for the food assistance currently provided seems unrealistic. As noted earlier, one of the important characteristics of the food-aid program is that it has greater support than other aid efforts because it directly serves domestic goals and promotes the interests of politically important groups who are not otherwise very internationally altruistic in outlook. On the one hand, if a serious effort were made to terminate food-aid programs, there is every reason to expect that substantial support could be mobilized among producers and humanitarian groups to counter such a move, however rational it might appear from a purely technical perspective. On the other hand, should such counter-efforts fail and food aid be actually terminated, there is little reason, based upon the recent politics of foreign aid, to expect that suspended food flows would actually be compensated for by increased cash flows. For these reasons, food aid is justifiably considered an additive to overseas development assistance rather than a substitution for what otherwise might be direct financial aid.

Among other reasons for a permanent (and development-oriented) food aid program is that it can continue to serve domestic farm and economic interests by reducing international price instability if it serves to expand the total volume of trade. This is especially important for American consumers and producers because of the minimum separation between American and international markets. A further reason rests on the notion that economic development in poor countries can serve American interests through the creation of greater market potential for all types of American goods, whether or not agricultural products, capital inputs to agriculture, or related goods. In recommending an indefinite continuation to food aid, we do not preclude terminating it at some time beyond the foreseeable future, that is, beyond the next ten to fifteen years. Indeed, a dole system of international welfare, of which food assistance is a prominent component, is not in itself intrinsically desirable, and a search for alternatives to it remains important. The overriding point is, however, that for the immediate future, larger, not smaller, flows of development assistance are needed.[12] Since food aid has a more substantial constituency than most other forms of overseas assistance, it is politically unrealistic to urge increased international assistance from the United States and at the same time promote the reduction or elimination of the food aid program.

Finally, aid in general, and food aid in particular, are desirable in American diplomacy. The strongest case for the general value of aid rests on an analysis of the needs of poor countries of the world. For most countries aid is thought to have had positive effects, both in fostering economic gowth and in creating a more peaceful and stable world order. The arguments for assistance, especially that which reduces rather than fosters dependency, have been argued forcibly by a number of studies, including those by John Montgomery, Robert Rothstein, David Wall, Charles Frank, Lester Pearson, and others, although various improvements, reforms, and additional measures are often recommended as well.[13]

The proposed development-oriented food-aid program, with food supplied on the basis of long-term commitments, perhaps even five years rather than the current step to three years, could even be used in tandem with long-term marketing arrangements in the commercial sector, mainly to help make more predictable market flows among producers and importers. Such a program would increase the desirability of having adequate reserves to meet obligations undertaken under long-term agreements. Farm policy and market-adjustment goals could still be served, but over a longer time frame than has been used in the past.

Priorities among Goals

How can competing goals and program priorities be resolved? One possibility is that amounts could be specified as allocated for each major purpose; for example, some proportion of food aid for political diplomatic objectives, another proportion for humanitarian, a third for developmental, and so forth. This would be an unwise step for two reasons. First, one of the important sources of support for the program is the fact that it can serve multiple, and distinctively different, interests at the same time. If, however, a particular proportion of food aid was distinctly labeled political, or distinctly labeled developmental or market promotion, then the coalition support would be subject to fragmentation. Furthermore, it is quite conceivable that any particular food-aid transfer would simultaneously serve two or more goals, as we discussed earlier in the case of Egypt. Equally difficult would be the situation where a proposal for food assistance to a particular country was turned down on developmental grounds, since it seemed likely to undercut rural development efforts, but was subsequently approved as a part of a political diplomatic program which operated independently.[14] In short, specifying objectives concretely and tying specific proportions of the food aid budget to them is very likely to reduce the level of support for the program in Congress and among the American public. At the same time, it would make it more difficult to administer aid programs without arbitrarily designating particular bilateral aid flows or having segments of the program working at greater cross-purposes to one another than currently.

The best solution in sorting priorities is to look to White House and congressional clarification of general priorities. During the years 1975 to 1978, it was clear that developmental and humanitarian objectives were designated by political leaders as the most pressing uses for which food aid is to be put. Once general priorities have been authoritatively established, implementation of food-aid decisions by senior officials at the working level should pose no serious problems. The resolution of trade-offs among conflicting policy goals becomes largely a matter of clarification of particular context and specification of probable outcomes from particular food aid agreements. Clearly officials who disagree strongly with the priorities set by Congress and the White House should discontinue their association with the food-assistance program.

The shift during the twenty years from 1955 to 1975 from dumping to development as the foremost objective of food aid is a welcome one. As long as food commodities are in surplus in the United States, supply-adjustment benefits of food aid can be derived for the American farm program with less conflict with other exporters since development food aid is more likely to be consumed by countries in serious balance-of-payment difficulties, countries most in need of development assistance, and by the portions of the population least able to enter commercial markets to secure needed nutrition. As suggested elsewhere, this emphasis on food aid will enhance America's ability to maintain a strong, positive, and morally correct image in the eyes of others, and to be in a position to supply important resources to Third

World countries seeking reform to the international economic system. Steps that would further institutionalize this priority include strong efforts to expand and improve the use of development-oriented provisions in current legislation (such as Title III), to interest more countries in Title III agreements, and to include food aid commitments more integrally in the analysis and planning of the Department of Agriculture and of Congress as they shape and execute domestic supply policies.

Can Assigning Priority to Development Really Work?

Recent studies by Uma Srivastava, Earl Heady, and others at Iowa State, by Hans Singer at the University of Sussex, and by Lester Gordon of Harvard, argue that food aid can be used for developmental purposes. The disincentive effects of food aid to local producers and upon those responsible for government development policy, they believe, can be minimized and, in the latter instance, even reversed.[15]

Beyond the conclusion that it is *possible* for food aid to serve developmental goals, both Congress and the president have clearly indicated their determination that it should be used to foster development to a greater degree than previously.

Food may have some important developmental effects that make it more desirable to use than cash. As Paul J. Isenman and Hans W. Singer point out, food aid is less readily appropriated by corrupt political officials for their personal use.[16] Furthermore, it is a commodity which the poor have a higher marginal propensity to consume (and need) and its addition to a country's stocks tends to benefit the poor. Moreover, it can lessen pressure on rural populations to supply urban areas with food, thus improving the diets of rural people indirectly if more food remains in the countryside. Of course, it can be of direct benefit when food is used in rural feeding programs or distributed in compensation for work on infrastructure development projects. In order to overcome criticisms of food aid's use to further

U.S. military goals, Congress passed legislation in 1975 that requires substantial emphasis (75 percent of Title I sales) to be directed toward the most needy countries. Congress has also enacted in 1977 the new Title III provision, which is geared for using food to assist in development plans by forgiving concessional sales repayments (Title I) if agricultural modernization efforts agreed to are in fact pursued. Although only three Title III programs had been established by mid-1979, a substantial possibility exists that if greater incentive structures are worked out (including paying shipping costs, guaranteed aid even during shortage periods, and limiting Title I availability where appropriate), the developmental and humanitarian aspects of this country's food aid can play a much larger role. If legislation does allow food aid commitments based on both humanitarian and development needs to be met regardless of the surplus situation in the United States, it would represent a substantial further transformation of food aid from its original surplus-disposal role. However, if long-term commitments are made under these conditions, more "reliable" supply policies in the United States may be needed. In particular, grain reserves, set-aside programs, and other government interventions will be called for to assure adequate supplies for Title III needs. One proposal for a 6 million ton wheat reserve, for instance, has been languishing in Congress during 1977–79 and would be especially helpful. A U.S. proposal for a 20 percent "over-call" on food aid commitment in the FAC was rejected by other donor states in 1978, but continuing U.S. efforts to improve the counter-cyclical character of food aid is needed. After all, as table 3.3 makes clear, the United States was the primary supplier responsible for cutting food aid during the period of greatest need in 1973–74. If such programs evolve, food aid will have come full circle from its inception, in which the dumping of surplus commodities was the primary objective, to a new situation in which development becomes the overriding desideratum of the program.

In actual practice, of course, the impact of food aid may not always be directly developmental, but it could assist development in a number of ways; providing better nutrition for rural workers; providing incentives for rural construction projects; providing insurance for farmers or governments that undertake new production strategies that promise higher yields but also entail increased risks; and providing food that can reduce balance-of-payments demands and release foreign currency for importing capital goods needed in a wide range of development projects. While it is clear that food aid could work in a variety of ways to assist development, it is not clear what in individual contexts would be satisfactory uses for furthering development, especially "equitable" development, which aims at raising the incomes and productivity of the rural poor rather than exacerbating inequality.

Keith Griffin has argued that land reform is an indispensable ingredient in strategies of rural development for many countries. MIT economist Lance Taylor likewise emphasizes political and social barriers to solving problems of equitable development and undernourishment of the rural poor. He argues that:

Some sort of income redistribution, through land reform, through disguised transfers via food or medical programs . . . , or through revolution is probably the most effective means of grappling with undernutrition. There is some hope for success, but it will come in decades and definitely not in the three-year time horizons of most foreign aid administrators and their advisers.[17]

We can accept the emphasis of these analysts, without accepting a prescription for revolutionary transformation of Third World countries. The point is fairly simple: whatever may be needed for rural modernization by way of agronomic technology in any country, a rural infrastructure that (1) brings peasants into the market, (2) provides access to the land, and (3) establishes a system of credit, education, and extension services is nearly always necessary. What form such restructuring of political and social institutions should take, and what type of "land reform" would be the most acceptable and effective will depend upon individual country contexts.

Before food aid can be used to support development efforts, including social and political changes, we need to have a better understanding of a number of factors. For one thing, can land reform and institutional reform be promoted through food aid? If so, how? Research to answer this question has, for the most part, yet to be done. It is possible, however, to specify some of the factors that need investigation. This includes the assessment of the noneconomic values of a society and an analysis of the distribution of benefits that currently reinforce existing social and political institutions among peasants. To the extent practical, additional quantitative values are desirable in order to expand policy analysis to include factors now regularly excluded from economic research. A list of such information needed to allow ongoing appraisals of the impact of food aid on development includes:

1. The distribution of productivity among farmers in major regions or countries where food assistance has been or will be sent;

2. Covariation in these areas of farmer productivity and major technical and social elements in production, i.e., size of land holding, amount of water available, patterns of credit, weather patterns, and production techniques (including seeds, multiple, double, and triple cropping, rotation and interseeding of crops, and so on);

3. Economic returns, both in crops and cash, to farmers, including portions appropriated through taxes or returned to creditors, landlords, and so on;

4. The relationship of the farming system to other forms of local economic activity, including trading, light industry, and local services;

5. The pattern of respect and accepted leadership in rural areas, that is, what are perceived sources of authority, and what kinds of behavior or attributes are accorded respect (e.g., is holding cattle of greater prestige than saving cash);[18]

6. The pattern of attitudes and level of technical understanding held at various levels within government organizations and their impact on the rural population, especially ministries of agriculture, land and resettlement, and public works;

7. Estimates of the costs of malnutrition in lost productivity and increased burdens on the health-care system (including informal health care provided by relatives of ill people who might otherwise be working). In order to understand the part that food assistance for development—and food delivery to nutritionally endangered or subsistence level populations—might play, we need to estimate the effect in increasing their capacity to work, to reason clearly, and to reduce demands on others for health care.

Organization for Program Implementation

The next chapter deals with the American government organization for coping with problems of interdependence in food. It is relevant here only to sketch out the distinctive features in the history of the organization of food aid programs and to indicate the general conclusions regarding government organization applicable to food aid. Since food aid is relevant to several aspects of problems, including reducing price instability in particular countries and regions, increasing long-term food supplies (through its developmental impact), and alleviating the suffering of malnutrition, the organization and implementation of food-aid programs must be closely intermeshed with the overall organization responsible for managing United States global food policies. Therefore, the argument regarding organizational recommendations is best left to the next chapter.

The Department of Agriculture and the Agency of International Development (and its predecessors) have been the principal agents for the administration of food aid. The Interagency Staff Committee (ISC), established by executive order during the Eisenhower administration shortly after the passage of PL480 legislation in 1954, has been until 1978 the mechanism for coordinating decisions on food aid. Although now called the Working Group of the recently established Sub-Committee on Food Aid, this body still brings together the full-time food-aid managers and does the staff work. From time to time, during periods of "crisis," aid decisions have been elevated to higher levels in the bureaucracy, as when President Johnson made monthly decisions on food aid to India during 1966–67 and when OMB and the Council of Economic Advisers (CEA) established committees in 1973–75 to oversee foreign agricultural policy, including food aid programs.

The ISC has been chaired by the Department of Agriculture (usually by the Assistant Sales Manager for PL480) with representatives from AID (the office of Food for Peace), Treasury, Commerce, State, OMB and Defense.[19] Since the initial thrust of the Act was "trade development" and the disposal of surplus commodities, it was natural for the Department of Agriculture to be the principal agency to execute the program . It had long been the lead agency administering these activities, as noted earlier, with gifts of food after the two world wars, and with concessional sales beginning in the 1930s. As the emphasis in food aid shifted to humanitarian and developmental objectives, the role of State and AID has increased. Secretary of State Dulles had little interest in food aid, under the Eisenhower Administration, other than preventing it from going to unfriendly or Communist countries.[20] In the Kennedy administration, George McGovern was appointed Food for Peace coordinator with a White House post, Title II programs (grants) expanded, and the role of AID—in administering Title II programs as well as participating in the initial foreign-country preparations of a request for Title I concessional sale—grew.[21]

With the passage of a four-year extension of the Food Aid Program in 1977, it is envisaged that Title III sales will increasingly supplant Title I sales, particularly if recent and pending legislation in fact guarantees Title III shipments priority during periods of world shortages and approves paying shipping costs.[22] The Agency for International Development and the Department of Agriculture in 1978 are in low-key dispute over who will run the Title III program. Agriculture can make a strong case that Title I and Title III food-aid shipments should both remain fully within its province, because of its important role in supplying credit via the CCC, administering the record-keeping for the program, and ultimately controlling which commodities are considered in surplus, and when this requirement can be waived out of humanitarian—and perhaps soon, developmental—considerations. In contrast, AID can also make a good case that it should run Title III programs, since the principal thrust of Title III is to encourage economic development and increased food production in less-developed countries, a mandate most closely associated with the Agency for International Development. The reorganization of food aid policy in 1978 did not settle this issue. The Food Aid Subcommittee of the intergovernmental group for development, the Development Coordinating Committee (DCC), is chaired by the Assistant Secretary of Agriculture for International Affairs and Commodity Programs, thus retaining a lead role for agriculture. The old ISC has become a "working group" of this Food Aid Subcommittee, with apparently somewhat less policy discretion.

One clear advantage of these new organizational arrangements is that the interagency principle, the recognition that multiple interests and multiple objectives are involved in food aid programs, continues to be recognized. Furthermore, while the ISC never had formal policymaking authority, such authority presumably will be given to the Food Aid Subcommittee, or at least to its parent body, which is chaired by the administrator of AID. While it is premature to assess the effectiveness of the reorganization in the spring of 1978, it conforms to the general principle of delegating decision-making authority to senior specialists. As other studies of U.S. government organization have concluded, policies that are run on a regular basis at the White House level or which attempt to impose imperatives from the

East-West conflict or other unidimensional perspectives on international affairs, overlook the needs of complex and unique local contexts, and have frequently been failures. This has certainly been true of failures in Angolan policy and of threatened food aid cutoff if East-West trade embargoes were violated, as by Bangladesh. President Johnson's effort to control food aid to India by personal decision each month during the 1966–67 shortages is another classic case of poor organization. Lloyd and Susan Rudolph have concluded that

> There is good reason to believe that a more routine handling of food aid policy for India in this period, i.e., greater reliance on normal diplomacy, at least would have avoided such costs (the discrediting of liberal economists and policymakers in India; the loss of Indian good will and harm to America's reputation for relatively disinterested humanitarian and developmental assistance) and might have secured some short-run and long-run benefits.[23]

The fact that the new (1977) Sales Manager in the Department of Agriculture for PL480, Fred Welz, has had substantial previous experience in AID, and that other Agricultural Department personnel, who, in general, support development as a priority are currently assigned to food aid, is extremely important. As numerous studies of organizational effectiveness have shown, the orientations and personal commitments of senior officials in the bureaucracy are an important element in the final foreign-policy outcomes.[24]

Multilateral versus Bilateral Food-Aid Channels

The last question raised in discussing the concessional food system is whether the United States should use bilateral or multilateral channels for sending food to others. This organizational issue is dealt with in a broader context and with fuller argumentation in chapter 5. Suffice it to note here, that U.S. bilateral aid has some multilateral aspects when consultations are made with other donor countries and/or with recipient countries. Thus, for example, in June, 1978, an aid "consortium" for Bangladesh was held in Paris, and included policy coordination for food aid. On the whole, however, such policy coordination is the exception and its occurrence is fairly recent. The bulk of U.S. participation in multilateral channels occurs under the World Food Program of the United Nations and FAO.

Food-aid supplies for the World Food Program come from the Title II (grant) budget of PL480. The proportion of American food aid is relatively small in such multilateral channels. In 1968, it amounted to less than 14 percent of Title II assistance and 2 percent of all U.S. food aid. Although contributions through the World Food Program multilateral channel slowly rose to 17 percent of Title II, this proportion has declined in the 1977–79 period largely because voluntary organizations such as Catholic Relief Services (CRS) and CARE have sought to maintain or increase the supply of food they have to distribute through various overseas programs; for them PL480 is very important because the government pays for the food, the cost of shipment, and even some overhead—support vital in their world-wide efforts.

There are some distinct advantages in multilateral channels, particularly with respect to imposing conditions which might seem onerous in a bilateral context. Indeed, the direct bilateral context may prove a substantial barrier to the negotiation of effective development and agricultural-production programs. To provide an alternative to U.S. initiatives, the World Food Program has indicated an interest in providing leadership in policy coordination among major donors (in accordance with Resolution 18 of the World Food Conference). Opportunities for expanding both the flow of food aid through multilateral channels, and for increasing the coordination of food aid and nonfood developmental assistance in order to maximize the potential for equitable development in Third World countries, should be attempted. In this regard, we suggest that the food-aid subcommittee of the Development Coordinating Committee (DCC) develop a liaison with the agricultural development program sponsored by the World Food Council and the Development Banks. Until recently the planning and policy-coordination (PPC) agency of AID has not sought to integrate official development assistance (ODA) flows in the form of food aid with project aid and technical assistance, except for the obvious cases of the Sahel and Bangladesh. Under new leadership in the PPC, interest in food aid has grown, and an effort to establish procedures for implementing a more inclusive analysis of food aid as part of overall development criteria, seems possible. This can be seen in the budgetary proposals for fiscal 1980 prepared at various overseas missions.

Conclusion

The American food-aid program, begun as emergency relief after World War I and as surplus-disposal practices in the 1930s, has evolved substantially into a set of development-oriented programs that seek to address both immediate nutritional needs and long-term development needs throughout the globe. The history of food aid in this respect is one in which Americans can take considerable pride. The concessional system of food flows in the world today has not only become institutionalized as a result of American initiatives and practices, but also has followed American policy leadership in moving toward more developmental and humanitarian purposes in making concessional transfers. In the future, food assistance can be relevant to the problems of global food interdependence in ways that go well beyond the pattern of interdependence initially encouraged and exploited through surplus disposal and sales to military allies that dominated the strategy of the United States in the late 1940s and 1950s.

CHAPTER 4

Organizing the Executive Branch for Foreign Food Policy

Until the "global food crisis" of 1973–74, the Department of Agriculture was the predominant agency in the United States government shaping both domestic and foreign food and agricultural policy.[1] This situation has changed. Although, under the Carter administration, Agriculture has once again regained substantial initiatives in setting American foreign food policies, it has done so for two reasons: first, the leadership in the department, under Secretary Robert Bergland and Under Secretary for International Affairs, Dale Hathaway, is more in agreement on international policy with the State Department (with a greater commitment to assisting agricultural development overseas), than it was in the Nixon/Ford administrations under Secretary Earl Butz. Second, we have returned to a period of relative surplus in food-exporting countries, especially the United States. Nevertheless, the growth of interdependence in food, the recognition of this (particularly after the tight supply situation in the early 1970s), and the pluralistic character of U.S. government—with its manifold interests and multiple arenas for decision-making—inevitably continue to require a large amount of coordination and compromise in arriving at any given policy.

The structural reasons for global interdependence have already been outlined. Similar reasons make various parts of the American society interdependent with respect to alternative food policies. As a reminder, recall that food is an important component in the Consumer Price Index (about 25 percent) and has been a major factor in the high inflation rates of 1974 and 1978–79. The lack of growth in agricultural earnings since 1975 (in constant dollars), compared to rising import costs, contributes to the record balance-of-payment deficits in 1978 and 1979, the decline of the dollar in the international money markets, and the pressure on the Federal Reserve to increase interest rates as a domestic monetary policy to alleviate this problem.[2] In addition, environmental and health concerns related to the use of fertilizers and chemicals in farming and grading and quality control related to marketing advantages, also involve various other interest groups in agriculture and food policy. While such broader domestic concerns are important, we only note the policy conflicts that directly affect foreign food policy and concentrate principally on the foreign policy issues.

Since 1972, substantial government reorganization has occurred in order to improve the balancing of interests and policy coordination. The multiple interests, and the economic interconnectedness, of different groups in our society affected in common by particular foreign policies help explain the existence of the many organizations that participate in shaping foreign food policy with its implications for domestic objectives of macroeconomic growth, low unemployment, and low inflation, and the international objectives of a favorable balance of trade, expanded trade that sustains general economic growth in the Western world, and the promotion of economic development and political stability in less-developed countries.

The most important bureaucracies shaping international food policy are in Agriculture and the State Department. The classic tension between the interests of farmers, who look to the Department of Agriculture as their spokesman, and the international goals which the Department of State necessarily forwards weigh heavily in assessments of the impact of American agricultural policy overseas.

The tension between these two interests—the one specialized, immediate, and intense, and the other more diffuse and long-term—can be seen in the management of overseas career posts which are the responsibility of the Department of State in most cases, but are controlled by the Department of Agriculture with regard to the foreign agricultural attachés. Few agricultural attachés have had diplomatic training or experience in the State Department, and yet they play an important role in shaping American foreign food policy. Situated in nearly seventy overseas posts and accredited to over one hundred countries, agricultural attachés can, and do, communicate directly to the Department of Agriculture information and recommendations for action (bypassing State altogether). While one of their primary functions is the promotion of the sale of American agricultural products abroad, they also file periodic assessments of overseas production and up-to-date news about developments in commercial markets. Nearly all attachés have received training in agricultural economics, principally at the major Midwestern agricultural universities, whose climate and departmental intellectual tradition is much more conservative than the Eastern and Far Western elite schools that disproportionately train foreign-service officers. The second tension among personnel in the policymaking organization is between specialists and generalists. The Department of Agriculture (and other functional departments such as Health, Education, and Welfare) are heavily staffed with specialists in nutrition, agronomy, and economics, while the economic bureau of the State Department, the Office of Management and Budget (OMB), and the Council of Economic Advisors (CEA) tend to have more generalists, people with fewer advanced degrees and more frequently degrees in liberal arts disciplines such as history and English.[3].

As the issues surrounding supply policy (set-aside requirements, income-support levels, and so on), and export policy—including sales to the Soviet Union, and food aid to the near-famine areas of the Sahel and Bangladesh—have become more complex, the locus of policy-making has tended to shift our agriculture policy increasingly into an interagency framework, away from specialists and more into the hands of generalists. From 1973 onward, agencies which before had usually only a marginal role to play in foreign food policy moved to expand their capability and role in decision-making. The State Department's Bureau of Economic and Commercial Affairs (E Bureau) expanded the size of its food policy division. The Treasury hired Hal Worthington, a specialist in foreign agricultural affairs,[4] and he brought in a supporting staff in 1973–74 to enable the Treasury to make independent estimates of world food conditions and possible impacts of these on domestic food prices. At OMB, the National Security Council (NSC) and the CEA similar growth in attention to food issues occurred. With the decline of saliency of food issues after 1975, there has been some attrition in the growth of these food speciality offices outside the Department of Agriculture. Nevertheless, there is a potential for many agencies to use a stake in food policy during periods of scarcity to renew their participation in the pulling and hauling of interests, with each major component of the bureaucracy defining food problems somewhat differently with respect to priorities and solutions. As figure 4.1 illustrates, the organizational response during the most recent period of food policy pressure was to create a variety of interagency and senior-level and working-level groups, each chaired by a different agency and each focusing on problems from a somewhat different perspective.

Standard Critiques and
Major Organizational Options

Nearly every analysis of the organization of food policy-making in the U.S. government has noted that a large number of agencies are involved in food policy. The General Accounting Office (GAO), for example, has described over seventeen U.S. government agencies in their extensive survey on the management of agricultural exports;[5] these multiple agencies have been accused of creating a labyrinth of conflicting signals and procedures.[6] The organization that existed in 1975 was accused of working at cross-purposes; it was argued that too

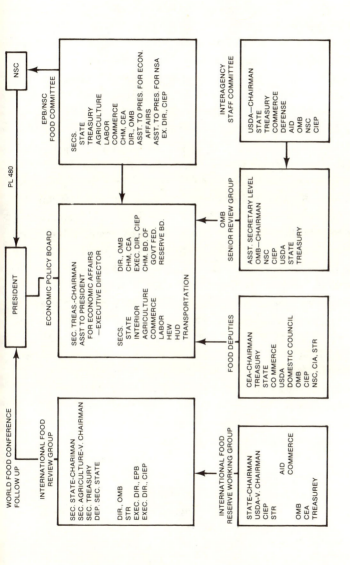

Figure 4.1

1975 Executive Office Organization for Food Issues

many agencies were involved and the result was too fragmented a set of policies. Indeed some critics argued there simply was no American foreign food or agricultural policy.[7] Research that would address international food problems for example, went forward under varying mandates within the Department of Agriculture, the Agency for International Development, HEW, the National Academy of Sciences, and the National Science Foundation. Trade policy was reviewed by OMB, Treasury, State, AID, and the President's Office of Special Trade Representative, as well as in at least two major branches of the Agriculture Department, the Foreign Agriculture Service (FAS) and the Economic Research Service (ERS—now ESCS). Critics, as we note in chapter 3, pointed out that during the period of acute shortage Agriculture's FAS was still emphasizing expanded exports and the Department of State was still trying to use food aid for political purposes even though the supply had been cut back to the point where famine conditions were inadequately met.[8]

Most of these organizational critiques overlook the fact that officials involved in the policy process are relatively well known to each other, have little trouble mastering the multiple interagency arenas within which policy discussions take place, and are generally aware of—if not empathetic with—the different interests and perspectives of others involved. Moreover, most efforts to "reorganize" have not been particularly successful. In 1976, President Ford appointed a single White House level food committee under the Economic Policy Board. This committee, chaired by Agriculture Assistant Secretary Bell replaced another committee chaired by the Department of State. The new group was supposed to (among other things) improve coordination and simplify decision making through a streamlined interagency body. In fact, the committee met infrequently and dealt with only a few topics, such as complaints about palm oil imports. This unspectacular outcome from organizational overhaul may have been the result of three factors: the impending 1976 election, which encouraged the postponement of major policy decisions; an increase in world grain supplies and substantial price reductions, with lessened fears of world shortages; and the lack of interest by the Agriculture Department in taking initiatives.

Reorganization Alternatives Considered

Since it is foolish to expect competing American and foreign interests and perspectives to disappear, the important question in considering organization is what would be the most effective structure both to allow for efficient decisions and to provide for each societal interest to be taken into account in policymaking. Among various reorganization proposals, three basic schemes exist. The first scheme is that of presidential leadership. It is argued that the interdependence of domestic and international food policy questions requires an interagency entity, established at the White House level and reporting to the President. The basic argument here is that important agricultural decisions, especially during periods of uncertainty or tight supply, will cut across the interests of a variety of government organizations and public interests, and can finally only be settled by someone in authority at the White House. Given this, a permanent standing committee is seen to be preferable to settling issues on an ad hoc basis, such as occurred during the early months of the Carter administration when set-aside targets for 1977 were established. As long as Treasury, OMB, the Council of Economic Advisers, the Special Trade Representatives (STR), the State Department, AID, and the NSC are all likely to see a substantial stake in decisions on domestic supply policy, as well as commercial and concessional export policies, a high-level institutionalized body that coordinates all these interests, while recognizing the important role of the Department of Agriculture, is a preferred solution.[9]

A second organizational recommendation, most persuasively argued by Edward A. Jaenke in congressional testimony and proposals to the Carter transition team in 1976–77 is to expand the role and scope of interest represented by the Secretary of Agriculture. One mode of accomplishing this would be to reorganize food policy into an expanded Department of Food and Agriculture. In this scheme, the Secretary of Agriculture would be not only the principal spokesman for farmers and other agricultural interests, but also for consumers and for importers of U.S. food products. Ideally, the Department of Agriculture, with its substantial and competent staff, and with food problems as a continuing focus of attention (in contrast to the sporadic levels of interest given food by the Departments of Treasury, State, and others), should be able to consider adequately national goals in making decisioins. To a large extent, the Carter administration has moved in the direction of Jaenke's proposal in three ways: individuals with greater international orientations and/or consumer interests have been recruited to senior posts in the department; agencies within the department have been regrouped so as to include a broader range of policy considerations under various Assistant Secretaries; and working relationships with other departments, notably the State Department and AID, in reaching international policy have been substantially improved. For example, during 1974–76, unrelenting tension existed between the departments of Agriculture and State over the desirability and form of an international grain reserve; under the Carter administration, however, the Department of State has been content to have Agriculture take the lead in shaping and negotiating an international grain reserve. This is because the policy positions and personnel of the Agricultural Department became largely congruent with those of the Department of State. Agriculture's 1978 position on international grain reserves, for instance, was nearly identical to positions promoted by the State Department, whereas in the earlier period the two departments were regularly in disagreement.

The final organizational alternative is to decentralize effective decisionmaking on particular policy to the "working level"; that is, to the Assistant Secretary level or below. This organizational alternative would delegate to senior officials in agencies whose perspective comes closest to the broad policy goals of the President and his advisers the lead responsibility for policy-making. This delegation need not necessarily transfer responsibility for policy implementation. This organizational strategy would continue and expand permanent interagency policy groups such as the Food Aid Committee of the Development Coordinating Committee (DCC) but would fall short of creating a permanent cabinet-level food committee. Rather, departments or agencies in strong disagreement with the lead agency could choose to use some of their bureaucratic "credits" by taking their disagreement to the White House for recognition. In this case, the Cabinet, subcommittee of the Cabinet, or an ad hoc senior-level group under the leadership of the President, would make a final decision. By making the White House level decision available only on ad hoc bases, the cost of raising issues to this level would be increased, the frequency of doing so decreased, and flexibility and innovativeness available to the working-level decision group would be enhanced. To be sure, important and difficult decisions would still require presidential authority, but each could be considered in the context of the decision itself, and with minimum impact on the standard operating procedures established by permanent White House staffs and interagency committees. Furthermore, this approach suggests that those with the greatest expertise in food policy, though perhaps representing different interests or vantage points, could more frequently be effective decision makers and less frequently look to the statutory authority or political standing of their "bosses," with the President as a basis for resolving issues. Moving complex issues to the Cabinet level does not necessarily enhance effective government. As one official in the Agricultural Department remarked, after attending a Cabinet-level meeting on food issues, "None of them knew what they were talking about, and yet there they were trying to make a decision."[10]

None of the three options outlined is mutually exclusive. All three recognize the need for a variety of agencies to monitor and regulate aspects of food policy. However, global food interdependence would be best addressed and managed, in our judgment, by emphasizing the third option outlined.

The Importance of Personnel
for Interdependence Policy-Making

The quality and orientation of senior personnel staffing the major departments and congressional committees that shape American food policy is an important factor in the organizational setting. The impact of interdependence, by increasing the competing pressures on officials (and thus making decisions less "overdetermined" by structural factors), has increased the importance that the personality and intellect of officials can have upon outcomes.

We take for granted that bureaucracy in a democracy will contain a multiplicity of interests. Further, given the checks and balances in the current system, a multitude of interests will continue to claim a stake in our foreign food policy. These interests will be served best by an institutional representation. Thus, Agriculture must continue to have a special concern for farmers. Indeed, if the farm and agribusiness communities no longer found the Department of Agriculture to be sympathetic to their concerns, and unable to share their perception of their interests, an important basis of political support for any administration and similarly *any* foreign policy would be lost. Since we believe that interagency coordination is unavoidable and is helpful in taking into account problems arising from food interdependence, certain features of personnel management are desirable. First, personnel within all agencies should be recruited who have a firm appreciation for the global context within which American policy resides; second, there should be increased long-range planning and management capability among senior personnel of the government. This latter task requires both improved intelligence gathering and analyses, and policy tools designed for securing longer-term benefits. A study of officials involved in shaping American international food policy in 1975 uncovered two characteristics of these officials. First, they formed a "network" in which informal channels of communication both among Americans in various parts of the government (including Congress), and with overseas counterparts, played an important role in shaping the positions taken in interagency forums and the final policy arrived at; secondly, these officials frequently had little diplomatic experience and held fairly narrow perspectives concerning global problems. Often they could not see longer-term indirect effects of policies, and hence were unable to address problems that might have longer-term substantial *costs* to the United States.[11] Our recommendations, consequently, are that some specialized personnel, in the Department of Agriculture, the State Department, AID, and the National Security Council (NSC) work together explicitly to develop longer-run (five- to fifteen-year) strategies for American foreign food policy. The economic/analytical skills of the Economics, Statistics, and Cooperative Service (ESCS) of the USDA should be combined with the skills in political analysis that reside in the policy-planning wings of the State Department, AID and the NSC. Such long-range planning should include five- and ten-year forecasts of likely American exports, both commercial and concessional, and the domestic supply policies most likely to produce adequate resources for such export needs. This special interagency policy analysis and planning unit should also assess the effects and value of long-term commodity arrangements such as the informal ones between the United States and Europe/Japan and the formal ones between the United States and the Soviet Union. In particular, the unit should complete its initial analyses prior to the negotiations needed in 1980 to renew or abort the U.S.-Soviet Grain Agreement.

Another subject this new unit should study is future export needs. Recall the predicted expansion in food import demand from less-developed countries (imports were up 17 percent from 1977 to 1978 alone) and their projected need of over 100 million metric tons of grain by 1990 (see chapter 1). In spite of protectionist policies which have reduced the trend of growing imports into EC countries, and the potentially slow growth of Japanese agriculture imports, future export prospects may be especially robust. However, the United States may fail to take advantage of, or respond adequately to, this future overseas demand. The growth rate in productivity in American agriculture has declined substantially. We had an 11 percent per annum growth rate in 1960–65 per unit of labor, and 3.7 percent per acre of production; this fell in 1971–75 to only 2 percent growth in labor productivity and 0.4 percent growth in acreage productivity.[12] Countries in the less-developed world are the ones experiencing the most rapid gains in productivity. Productivity growth rates, for all factors of production, are occurring among some LDC's at 3 percent to 4 percent. If these productivity gains continue, and if population growth subsides, thanks perhaps to control efforts already begun, it is probable that a new group of exporting countries may begin to compete with the United States. Already Brazil and Pakistan are entering export grain markets; these may merely be harbingers of a more general phenomenon. Large gains in agricultural production in less-developed countries should, of course, be welcomed for their overall positive impact on economic development and political stability, not to mention expanding the market for American and Western world nonagricultural products. Nevertheless, domestic supply policy must be geared to adjust to such changes, trying to be able both to meet world food needs if shortages arise, and, at the same time, to retain sufficient adaptability to meet potential competition from countries with more labor-intensive technology.

A second recommendation, aside from the policy analysis unit, would be to use recruitment to encourage greater appreciation and understanding of global concerns among senior officials. This will require, among other things, changing recruitment and promotion criteria somewhat to give greater value for experience in more than one agency. Possibly appointments to senior posts should be screened on an interagency basis. Further, within the State Department and AID, personnel assignments should be extended in order to allow development of greater specialization among senior officials. This has been accomplished to some extent in the office of Food for Peace in AID (though with practically no upward mobility), but in the State Department and the Planning and Program Coordination Bureau of AID continuity is far weaker. From 1975 to 1978, for example, three different foreign service officers have headed the "Food for Freedom" division (a title changed to "Food Programs" in 1978) within the Economic Bureau of the State Department. For food interdependence, in particular, and for the successful management of global economic issues, in general, personnel in regional bureaus, of necessity, must become somewhat more administrators and less coordinators of policy. Assignments in functional bureaus must play a greater role in promotional ladders and, in general, State Department norms should come to reflect the mission of the department in which the task of good relations among states is given somewhat less weight than that of the management of global problems. Such management, as indicated above, must occur through interagency coordination and cooperation with the domestic and international officials of various other departments of the U.S. government, particularly the Departments of Agriculture and Treasury.

Accommodating External Interests in Internal Executive Branch Relations

In 1973 with the soybean embargo (which shocked the Japanese and Western Europeans), in 1974 with the suspension of grain sales to the Soviet Union, and again in 1975 with the suspension of sales to Poland and to the Soviet Union until the October 1975 grain agreement was reached, we witnessed three dramatic episodes of bureau-cratic politics within the administration. In each instance, the out-come was undesirable in some respects, and, in each, White House level intervention occurred to adjust policies that seemed adrift. Because firmer steps were not taken at intermediate interagency levels, and because major interest groups, particularly consumers and trade unions, were alarmed about export policies, sporadic interven-tions into policy at White House level occured.[13]

Joseph Gavin's close analysis of export policy-making of 1974 suggests that the bureaucratic struggles among various agencies were principally a reflection of larger societal-interest-group conflicts. "The actors and the tactics were bureaucratic, but the outcomes were determined by the latent balance of interest group pressures and the 'lessons of history.'"[14] Since such interest-group pressures in a democ-racy require sympathetic and adversarial representatives within the executive branch, the hope for greater continuity and foresight in managing the American supply and export policies requires an inter-agency framework with continuity and authority. Executive leader-ship ideally should provide the broad guidelines for policymaking by determining priorities and articulating fundamental goals, and the executive branch should recruit personnel who share their policy views and who are professionally competent. The sharp conflicts that arose within the Nixon-Ford administration highlight the need for an interagency framework in which broader interest conflicts are appre-ciated, and in which compromises that follow the broad policy guide-lines of the incumbent administration can be reached. The principle of unanimity in interagency councils seems too stringent. For exam-ple, the Interagency Staff Committee (ISC) that managed the details of food aid from the Eisenhower to the Carter years was rather ineffective in making PL 480 decisions when food aid allotments were cut back. This is because the situation required hard choices, and because of the unanimity rule, in part; and because of the attention given food issues, more senior review groups emerged to take over food-aid management.

That the machinery of American food diplomacy reflects some perhaps irreconcilable conflicts in our foreign policy, both in the substance and procedures, is unsurprising. Policy, nevertheless, even if only the de facto failure to act, will be made. The interagency framework provides the best hope for effective policy-making, if personnel within it represent both a spectrum of interests and also embrace an understanding of the broader global context within which they are operating. As we argued earlier, this organizational emphasis, plus a clear delegation of authority to a lead agency, is best for minimizing the social dislocations and domestic political repercussions of foreign food policy; and it also offers the best hope of minimizing the need for periodic White House intervention that inevitably carries substantial costs in diverting the attention of top policymakers.

In summary, the interagency framework option should attempt to reconcile the conflicts:

1. Between commercial-economic interests and noneconomic political and humanitarian concerns;

2. Between domestic and foreign interests;

3. Between centralized command and control to increase coherence and the efficiency gained by delegation of authority;

4. Between calculations of global effect and bilateral considerations of United States relations with particular trading partners or food-recipient countries;

5. Between immediate costs and dislocations and long-term benefits and costs.

Such a balancing of interests, while difficult, is both required and possible. The key ingredient is recruitment and the rewarding of personnel within the various agencies who have the confidence, breadth, and delegated responsibility to undertake the balancing task.

A final word is in order about Congress. Congressional reviews of food-aid policy, export policy notably with the Soviet Union, and supply policy, particularly the determination of acreage set-asides, play an important role in establishing and shaping the executive branch framework within which food policy can be carried out. There seems virtually no hope that the jurisdictional distribution of responsibilities between the foreign policy committees (the House International Relations Committee and the Senate Foreign Affairs Committee), the Agricultural Committees and the Appropriations Committees will be substantially altered in the forseeable future. Increasingly, the international committees have heightened their interest in our food diplomacy, to a point where the most recent four-year renewal of food aid—the International Development and Food Assistance Act of 1977—was reviewed in the House by both the International Relations and Agricultural Committees (though only by Agriculture in the Senate). Substantial reorganizations in the executive branch have regularly been minimized and sometimes completely prevented by Congress, which is reluctant to see its influence over particular agencies shifted through reorganization, thereby shifting the assignments of established congressional committees.[15] Ties between committee staff and various executive branch officials make major shifts in food responsibilities unlikely.

During the 1972–76 period, congressional overview proved a particularly important stimulant to the bureaucracy. Congressional initiatives limited most food-aid use to those most needy, and they pushed Agriculture toward adopting a policy of full production. It was virtually impossible, thanks to congressional legislation and pressure, to use crop set-asides from mid-1973 until 1977.

Subsidiaries of Congress, such as the Office of Technology Assessment (OTA) and the General Accounting Office (GAO) also have a hand in executive branch policy-making. These arms of Congress mounted in 1974–75 a series of studies investigating American food research capabilities, intelligence operations, and internal management of export policy, particularly the Russian grain sales. Such studies contributed in important ways by enhancing the understanding of complex policy issues by those involved in agricultural policy, by exposing questionable practices as in export grading and sales monitoring, and by promoting a series of recommendations that have helped lead to greater efforts in research, in intelligence gathering, and in managing export policies. Many of these recommendations have been adopted by the Carter administration.

To understand fully the organizational framework for food diplomacy, it is also necessary to mention the role of major producers and commodity interest groups. For example, at the Multilateral Trade Negotiations in the spring of 1978, chief negotiator Dale Hathaway included among his advisers specialists from the wheat associations, such as Michael Hall of Great Plains Wheat, and others representing the major grain-trading interests or firms. One representative of hunger groups, Brennon Jones of Bread for the World, had been consulted, but no representatives from the voluntary agencies distributing food aid were included. When pressed concerning the presence of representatives of commercial interests, USDA officials defended this on the basis that commercial representatives were the most informed and knowledgeable about particular details and problems that would arise in working out an international reserve policy or in reaching politically acceptable agreements on a national stockpiling and pricing policy.[16] In general, this claim and practice are neither novel (they were certainly practiced in the Ford administration and earlier) nor challenged seriously. The fact is that there is a close interrelationship between public and private sectors in these areas and, whether for good or ill, public bureaucrats depend heavily upon analyses and information provided by the private sector.[17] (Food aid groups such as CARE and CRS participate, but largely through collaboration with AID officials, and hence do not directly affect food supply and trade policy-making.)

Our recommendation is *not* that such relationships should be truncated, but that they should become more public and more representative, and that where interagency decisionmaking proves to be effective and authoritative, representation of these interests by sympathetic bureaucrats, or by other modes, should be fully open to congressional and public scrutiny. In short, we recommend democratization of the policy process with a delegation of authority to working-level specialists and senior professional personnel, who worry full time about food diplomacy problems at the level of Assistant Secretary and below.

CHAPTER 5

American Multilateral Food Diplomacy: The United States Role in International Organizations

The United States participates in a myriad of international organizations concerned with problems of the global food system. Eighty-nine international intergovernmental bodies were recently listed in a report on American organizational activities in world food affairs prepared by the United States Senate.[1] If one were also to count the private associations that include American members, our multilateral involvements in international food trade, aid, research, education, and communication would number in the thousands. Needless to say, it would be a large task, well beyond the scope or intent of this chapter, even to begin to map the full structure of the international organizational arena for food, and even lengthier efforts would be required to assess in any detail the specific operations and impacts of these countless bodies. While we do present some broad structural mapping and organizational evaluation, the main point of this chapter is to explore the relationship between American interests and past and future American participation in international organizations dealing with food questions. In this regard, we shall be paying special attention to American dealings with the United Nations Food and Agricultural Organization (FAO).

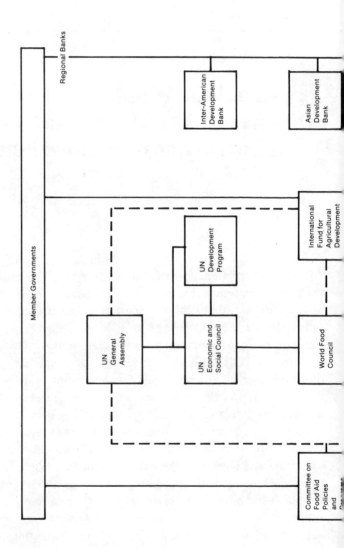

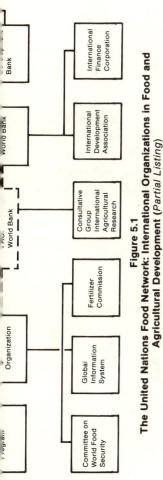

Figure 5.1

The United Nations Food Network: International Organizations in Food and Agricultural Development (*Partial Listing*)

The most important recommendation that emerges from this analysis is an urging toward more active, coordinated, and positive United States participation in food organizations.

International Food Organizations

With the special exception of organizations instituted to monitor and regulate international dealings in particular agricultural commodities, and the notable exception of the General Agreement on Tariffs and Trade (GATT), the most important international organizations involved in food affairs are all elements of the United Nations system. Central among these is the United Nations Food and Agricultural Organization. FAO is an autonomous association, linked to the United Nations system by agreement between the FAO Conference and the General Assembly in 1945. It is responsible only to its members (currently 136 national governments) and is financed by them for its regular budget, which largely pays for headquarters costs and staff operations.[2] The charter mandate of FAO calls upon it: (1) to collect, analyze, and disseminate information relating to food and agriculture; (2) to provide an international forum for consideration of food problems; and (3) to provide technical assistance to member countries, all with the ultimate object of "ensuring humanity's freedom from hunger."[3]

Most closely bound to FAO (or vice versa) within the UN system is the United Nations Development Program (UNDP). (See figure 5.1.) The main source of technical assistance in the UN, UNDP was founded in 1966 through a merging of the Expanded Program of Technical Assistance (EPTA) and the United Nations Special Fund. FAO currently serves as the executing agency for most projects in food and agricultural development financed by UNDP, and UNDP reimbursements yearly constitute the single largest category of FAO's total receipts—about double that of the regular budget of $106 million (for 1978).[4]

Less intimately associated with FAO, but still importantly

linked, are the World Bank Group, the three regional development banks, the World Food Program, and other "cooperative" programs. Through a World Bank/FAO Program, FAO assists the Bank in identifying and evaluating projects for possible funding, and it aids prospective loan recipients in preparing applications. Less direct links have existed between FAO's Industry Cooperative Program, its Investment Center, and the Bank's International Finance Corporation, where liaison and exchanged information guide private-sector investments in food processing and agricultural development. By way of their capital-raising activities, and via intraprofessional communication, the World Bank Group is connected to the Inter-American Development Bank (IDB), the Asian Development Bank (ADB) and the African Development Bank (AFDB), all of which finance agricultural development.

The World Food Program (WFP), created in 1962, is essentially an international food-aid operation that principally finances projects, funding, and development with food and modest overhead support pledged by members. WFP also intermittently functions to supply disaster and famine relief (about 10 percent to 15 percent of its outlay), working with the UN Disaster Relief Office. Organizationally, it is linked to FAO via appointments to its governing body, via cooperative field operations, and via having its main offices at FAO headquarters, where FAO provides heavy staff support (for which WFP reimburses FAO). Cooperative programs also link FAO to various other parts of the UN system; these include a program with the World Health Organization (WHO) on food standards (the Codex Alimentarius Commission), a program with the United Nations Children's Fund (UNICEF) directed toward improving nutrition among children, and a program in education about global hunger and food needs, the Freedom From Hunger Campaign.

Several new organs were created by the World Food Conference in November, 1974, and these are now operating in the UN food network. Resolutions approved first by the Conference and later by the UN General Assembly established a World Food Council (WFC) as the "highest" institution on world food problems in the UN system. Meeting at the ministerial level, the WFC is composed of 36 countries, nominated by the Economic and Social Council (ECOSOC) and responsible to it.[5] Its composition represents a world fragmented into an industrialized North, an underdeveloped South, a capitalist West and a socialist East. For broad policy issues, the WFC was intended to be the hub of the UN Food Network. Whether it will achieve this status remains to be seen. After an initial conflict over personnel and budget for operations, the WFC has had two meetings (1977 and 1978) that elevated substance above rhetoric. The assessment of progress at its Fourth Annual Meeting in Mexico City, June, 1978, suggested that many of the goals of the Rome Food Conference (1974), which the WFC was to shepherd into existence, had not been realized in part or at all.[6] According to conference reports, the 10 million ton minimum food-aid goal was barely reached, the grain reserve seemed unlikely to succeed, and many other steps to alleviate hunger had not reduced the number of people who eat too little— well below minimum standards. Since 1978, the WFC Secretariat has put most of its lobbying and coordinating capability into efforts to improve poor-country food supplies through rural development. Its clearest success was in the adoption of national food system studies as agreed to and funded at its 1979 meeting in Ottawa.

Also authorized at Rome in November, 1974 was the International Fund for Agricultural Development (IFAD). After an initial capitalization of just over $1 billion had been raised, the IFAD began operations in 1977 with the special aim of helping the poorest of the less-developed countries. It reports to, but is not an authority under, the Secretary General of the UN, and its operations are overseen by a governing board composed of representatives of three categories of countries—developed donor, developing donor (e.g., OPEC) and developing recipient.[7] It has a complex voting system and thus far relies on the major development banks to assist in project appraisals.

Established in 1969, the Consultative Group on International Agricultural Research (CGIAR) is an international consortium of donor and recipient governments, development banks and private foundations, sponsored by FAO, the World Bank and the UNDP. It functions to support and coordinate the activities of eleven agricultural research centers specializing in problems of food production in less-developed countries, and it administers a budget for them of over $80 million (in 1978).[8] As with the IFAD, representation to the CGIAR by the United States government is under the aegis of the Agency for International Development (AID) but the State Department, Treasury, and Agriculture all expect to be consulted and all attempt to shape U.S. participation.

In addition to organs already described, there are several UN bodies that regularly consider food questions as aspects of their broader programs. Significant among these is the United Nations Conference on Trade and Development (UNCTAD), where intense debate has centered on North-South trade issues, many having to do with terms of trade for agricultural commodities and commodity agreements as discussed in chapter 2.[9] In many ways, UNCTAD has become as salient a forum for North-South agricultural issues as has GATT for developed Western states bargaining on agricultural issues.

Some words of caution are in order before we move from this quick "mapping" into analysis and evaluation. First, organizations depicted in figure 5.1 and briefly highlighted here are by no means a complete list of international food bodies, not even as regards the UN network. For one thing, there are various coordinating committees and ad hoc food groups interlaced among the major institutions, such as the Committee on Surplus Disposal (CSD) of FAO which monitors concessional sales for possible violations of antidumping norms. For another, many of the major organizations noted, FAO in particular, contain any number of quasi-autonomous, differentially responsible organs within them. Second, the operational world of the groups and associations of the UN system is not nearly as orderly, well-organized, or separate as figure 5.1 indicates, or as the discussion suggests. In reality, redundancy (for good or ill) is rampant, complementarity is often unrecognized or at least unexploited, responsibility is poorly defined as is accountability, coordination is difficult, and political and bureaucratic activities buttress institutional autonomy and proliferation to add further complications to the network. Third, let us caution against mistaking activity for impact or accomplishment. There is a good deal of activity surrounding the international organization of food affairs, but budgets are modest, authority is limited, support from member states is tentative, and, for myriad political and bureaucratic reasons, including a strong imperative not to tamper with the sovereign integrity of any state, organizations tend to be restrained from accomplishing their mandated tasks.[10]

American officials and political leaders in recent years have increasingly found international organizations inhospitable. The voting majorities for U.S preferences in the United Nations have long eroded, actions against Israel and South Africa and other issues have caused the United States to leave the International Labor Organization, to threaten to abandon UNESCO, and to complain about the strident and unproductive rhetoric in many other forums. This skepticism has been less for FAO than for other bodies, but the United States has nonetheless sought to avoid the strongest demands arising in these meetings and has encouraged smaller groups to work out international food questions whenever possible.[11] U.S. preference for moving the discussion of reserves to London and to the International Wheat Council is a case in point. (See chapter 2.)

International Organizational Functions and Food Affairs

It is, however, generally ill-advised for American leaders to evaluate international institutions in terms of unrealistic and historical criteria. Many global food problems could be more effectively addressed if international organizations were more authoritative, more efficient, more respected in the eyes of member governments, more preferred as diplomatic arenas, and more able to command the resources required for fulfilling their objectives. Yet, rather than dwell upon functions international organizations do not, and perhaps cannot, perform, or perform ideally, given the environment in which they operate, note should be made of the functions they can and do perform in international food affairs. It is in this "realistic" analysis of the functional context of international organizations that we can best evaluate the advantages of United States participation.

In our estimation, at least five important functions in world food affairs are well served by existing international organizations. They are each deserving of American encouragement and support.

1. *International organizations as locations for consultation and international education.* The congresses, conferences, and committees of international organizations are first and foremost meeting places where national leaders or their representatives can come together to exchange views. If they did not exist, imperatives for international communication would invariably create them. Forums provided by international food institutions range from massive international conferences such as the World Food Conference in November, 1974, or the biennial conferences of FAO, which set themes and tones for subsequent food diplomacy, to small seminars for experts where detailed questions are debated and technical information is exchanged. In fiscal 1975, for example, American officials attended 77 international organizational meetings related to food and agriculture. More than 240 American delegates were involved at a cost of approximately $340,000.[12] Estimated costs incurred in preparing for such international meetings were in the neighborhood of $1.6 million.[13] Most involved in these international forums deemed them important and worth the costs in time and money they entailed. For example, when asked to cite benefits to the United States from participation in FAO, former Assistant Secretary of Agriculture Richard Bell told a Senate subcommittee that the first benefit was in

providing forums [in which] agricultural, fisheries, food and forestry policy and technical problems are discussed with representatives of other countries .... Through them it [the United States] obtains a great deal of useful information, develops better understanding or agreement with other countries on problems of common concern and contributes to improved international relations generally.[14]

This view was also stressed during the same Hearings by Samuel W. Lewis, former Assistant Secretary of State for International Organization Affairs:

On the benefit side, the greatly increased [FAO] membership provided a forum for balanced consideration, in most cases of problems which too often in the past had been considered in isolation. A global economy becoming steadily more interdependent made such dialogue indispensable. FAO sessions, particularly technical meetings or seminars in developing countries, have provided many opportunities for exerting United States influence on a large variety of agricultural matters of interest to us.[15]

There is no clear evidence to suggest that organizational forums enhance international cooperation, that they render issues more tractable than they might be otherwise, or that they facilitate agreement more readily than bilateral dealings. In fact, the contrary is probably true, inasmuch as discussions within international organizations tend to politicize technical issues, complicate simple ones, and unaccountably simplify complicated ones. Nevertheless, international discussion in organizational forums does raise consciousness about the gravity of issues, and it exposes all governments to the views, perspectives, and logics of all others. As such, it promotes international insight. In addition, interactions in organizational arenas generate information essential to national policy-making, and the emphases and urgencies exhibited at international gatherings directly influence national agendas and focuses of policy attention. Furthermore, since the governments of a great many less-developed countries currently prefer to conduct most of their international relations via multilateral organizations, business carried on in preparation for, during, and in response to their meetings and conferences is bound to become an increasingly large proportion of the total substance of international relations. What is generally true in this regard for global affairs will be particularly true for food and agriculture affairs, since this area is already one of the most highly organized internationally.

2. *Initiative and prodding.* Through reports, multilateral conferences, speeches by officers, good offices and other means of quiet diplomacy, international organizations often persuade or prod member governments to confront issues or consider policy options that national officials might otherwise choose to ignore. Here, there are any number of recent cases in point. Latest impetus for the idea of an international grain reserve, for example, came from a 1973 proposal by former FAO Secretary-General Boerma.[16] The scheme contradicted American and Canadian policies at the time,[17] but the international attention it attracted, and the domestic support it received outside of the U.S. government, prompted reconsideration and review, and Boerma's initiative became one of the elements that brought a change in the American position by 1974.[18] Even more telling as an example of the impacts of international organizational prodding are some of the results of the World Food Conference in 1974. Despite the political polemics and apparent obduracy of many national positions expressed in Rome, the themes of impending scarcity, food security, and greater self-sufficiency via rural modernization, emphasized in preparatory documents drafted by the FAO staff, subsequently became paramount issues in food diplomacy and important inputs into LDC national planning.

3. *Accumulating and disseminating information via organizational activities.* By collecting information, fostering professional communication, and sponsoring research, international organizations provide valuable services that national governments might either take little interest in, or forgo because of the high costs involved. As the principal intergovernmental organization for food

affairs, FAO reviews and reports upon nearly all international activities in the field.[19] It also extensively monitors national agricultural conditions as well as the global status of forests and fisheries. Only the research activities and output of the United States Department of Agriculture are in any way comparable to FAO's information programs, as only these two sources comprehensively depict global conditions. Only FAO materials are universally disseminated. FAO's budgets for research and publication are small compared to amounts spent by governments for nationally focused programs. Yet, the organization's output is substantial; its periodicals, yearbooks, and country analyses are frequently cited, and its projections frequently guide national planning and policy-making.[20]

The network of institutions involved in international agricultural research is centered in FAO, but it extends beyond it to include other public organizations, such as national research and development agencies including the United States Agency for International Development and Canada's International Development Agency (CIDA). It also includes a number of quasi-public bodies, such as the eleven international research centers coordinated by the Consultative Group on International Agricultural Research.[21] Widespread international communication about agricultural research is a development of the last two decades, primarily fostered by international organizations. While a full assessment of the institutions in this area is premature, it is fair to credit cooperative international research ventures during the 1960s with producing the "miracle seeds" for high-yielding dwarf varieties of wheat and rice that led to what some proclaimed as a "Green Revolution" in food production.[22]

4. *Assistance and advice.* International organizations operating in the food and agriculture field have become increasingly involved in funding rural development, technically assisting national governments, and otherwise conducting field operations designed to contribute directly to improving agricultural and nutritional conditions in underdeveloped regions.[23] The list of activities engaged by FAO

directly and as agent for the UNDP, by other specialized agencies of the United Nations including the World Health Organization and UNICEF, by UNDRO, the WFP and the World Bank Group, is much too lengthy to begin to elaborate. However, three points concerning development-assistance efforts on the part of multilateral agencies are important. First, these have been expanding rapidly over the past several years, so much so, in fact, that FAO's budget for field activities now far exceeds its regular budget. The organization, especially at the urging of its current Director-General, Dr. Saouma, has become increasingly a development-assistance institution.[24] Second, development assistance (and other services) performed by international organizations often take the form of activities that national governments will not, or cannot, perform for political reasons. For example, activities deemed interventionist or "imperialistic" if attempted on a bilateral basis are often acceptable to host governments if attempted by multilateral agencies. Similarly, countries that might be denied assistance on the basis of the ideological concerns, or political priorities, of leading national donors often find international organizations sympathetic to their proposals and needs. Third, in recent years there has been a rethinking and re-targeting of aid and technical assistance given by international organizations toward greater emphasis on the interests and needs of small farmers in poor countries.[25] The World Bank in particular has greatly increased the proportion of development assistance lent for improving the lot of the poor through agricultural and rural development assistance. Lending grew from $944 million in fiscal 1974 to $3,270 million in 1978 and is projected to increase by 50 percent more in real terms by 1983.

5. *International legitimacy and imprimatur.* International organizations can, and do, influence international relations (and national policies) in food and agriculture by legitimating practices and patterns, thereby often turning them into norms. The decisions of international organizations tend, as a rule, to evoke deference (even when

they are honored in the breach), and the imprimatur "multilateral" tends to heighten the acceptability of practices prescribed for some governments by others. Moreover, the legitimacy and force of prescriptions by international organizations is not limited only to treaties, conventions, and other formal acts of international law making, but to resolutions, expressions of multilateral consensus and even to views, recommendations, and espoused doctrines of high-level international civil servants.[26] Relevant examples of multilateral legitimation include UN and FAO efforts to shape "development" into an international responsibility, GATT's strengthening of free-trade principles in the international commercial system, and FAO's endorsement of the principles of the freedom of agronomic information and the transnational basis of agricultural research. It is not surprising that many principles and practices legitimated by international organizations are often simply multilateralized versions of policies and preferences of powerful member states, as was for example, FAO's endorsement of American positions on the legitimacy of surplus disposal via food aid.[27] Achieving such multilateralization is indicative of exercising leadership within organizations. In addition, there is something to be said for the importance of international organizations, and their capacities to legitimize, as states go about seeking foreign-policy instruments. As preferences for diplomacy through international organizations become more pronounced, seeking multilateral imprimatur should become an increasingly important and efficacious foreign-policy stratagem.

American Interests and World Food Organizations

As reported earlier, American support for international food organizations, most notably FAO, has declined in recent years. This has coincided with the increased activity of the poorest states in the United Nations, where various agencies charged with international welfare tasks have become primary arenas of debate between advocates of a New International Economic Order and their critics, notably including the United States. As many practices in global food trade and aid have become subject to increasing challenge, stress, and deviation—and as these have often been articulated vitriolically in organizational forums—political leaders in the United States (and other industrialized countries) have reacted defensively to protect their perceived stakes in the traditional status quo. Part of their strategy has been to deflate universal multilateral bodies, and hence to dampen "populist" pressures by circumventing forums controlled by Third World majorities. Alternatively, American spokesmen have sought to create (or revitalize) smaller specialized institutions with built-in veto opportunities, weighted voting, limited membership or limited authority, and to propose bilateral alternatives to multilateral programs, where "one-on-one" rather than "one-against-many" bargaining conditions would prevail. Simultaneously, the stances of the United States and allied industrialized countries in the larger multilateral forums have either hardened against reform, or shifted into defensiveness, delay, and waffling.[28]

To the extent that such a retreat from leadership in food organizations has characterized United States behavior in recent years, intentionally or not, it should be reversed. Two lines of reasoning support this conclusion.

First, *the current directions and policies of major food organizations complement U.S. policies and further U.S. goals.* If major statements of American foreign agricultural policy—and declarations concerning our overseas development policies more generally— are reliable descriptions of our goals, then it must be recognized that many world food organizations are targeted in directions we clearly prefer. For example, calls for more emphasis upon self-sufficiency through rural modernization in the Third World put forth by American officials and endorsed by the World Food Conference, are currently reflected in the enhanced development activities of FAO, in the newly kindled rural development interests of the World Bank Group, in the World Food Council's prevailing concerns with "food security," in the plans and early allocations of the International Fund for Agricultural Development, and in the expanded resources and efforts of the World Food Program. Relatedly, American interest and emphasis upon rural reform in the interest of poor farmers in poor countries, as reflected currently in Title III provisions in PL 480 and more traditionally contained in guidelines for the Alliance for Progress and other U.S. assistance programs, is at the center of FAO concern and World Bank, WFP, and IFAD planning.

In a similar manner, American concern for enhanced world food production through agronomic research and technological innovation is matched by endorsements for research affirmed at the World Food Conference, and strengthened programs and funding via CGIAR. President Carter's election-campaign calls for making the United States the breadbasket, not the arms merchant, of the world, have not only been followed up in specifics by the United States, as in Washington's more aggressive efforts to get larger food aid commitments, or in the 6 million ton emergency reserve before Congress since 1977, but these have also found counterpart articulations in the deliberations of the World Food Council and in multilateral negotiations surrounding the renewal of the International Wheat Convention. They are also contained historically in FAO's design for a World Food Authority and more recently in that organization's 1975 endorsement of an "International Undertaking on World Food Security."[29]

With regard to the international commercial system for food, current GATT concerns, reflected in the MTN agenda, about abusive marketing practices and nontariff barriers to agricultural trade accord well with American interests.[30] FAO studies on Agricultural Adjustment have tried to pinpoint areas where trade barriers might possibly be reduced.[31] Additionally, FAO's creation of an "early warning" mechanism and steps taken in Rome to enrich and expedite reporting on crop and marketing conditions also complement American interests and needs.

American concerns for humanitarian food distributions and the nutritional upgrading of diets among the world's poor are promoted by the World Food Program, the World Health Organization, the United Nations Disaster Relief Organization, and other organizations currently moving to mobilize and systematize food aid globally.

To indicate convergences and congruences between American goals and the programs of international organizations is perhaps both obvious and also beside the point. Many of the international programs noted are in fact the past fruits of American leadership and their relationship to American preference is therefore hardly surprising. Moreover, it is not so much these programs that are the sources of present American dismay with the organizations, but rather pending and accomplished changes in the authority and procedures of the institutions themselves. High politicization and ideological conflict characteristic of North-South relations in recent years have penetrated the food institutions, and the LDC's clamoring for "participatory democracy" has indeed fouled multilateral decision making. United States frustrations in this new international political setting are real. Still, is opting out of a game that looks so promising in its potential outcomes preferable to learning patiently how to play it better? If American interests really rested in maintaining a concentration of decisional influence in international organizations that is unreflective of the distribution of global influence, or in defending a status quo biased against the Third World, or in instituting an empire founded on "food power," then withdrawal toward unilateralism might be in order. But, if these latter are not American interests, there is little to be lost, and a great deal to be gained with regard to our substantive interests in global food trade and security, by adjusting tactics and positions in institutional forums and better supporting promising multilateral programs.

Second, *international organizations provide promising arenas and instruments for the pursuit of American food goals.* Another strand in reasoning to a recommendation for positive American participation in international food organizations concerns limitations on the United States' capacities to accomplish ends unilaterally. It is not necessarily the case that American power in world affairs has declined, at least not in world food affairs. Indeed, this country continues to command both the resources and the allocative flexibility to support an active and effective foreign policy, and in the food sector our resources are even more abundant than during the heyday of ascendance during the 1950s and 1960s. Moreover, our vulnerabilities in global food affairs that stem from dependence upon commercial markets are likely to remain more theoretical than real as we move toward the predicted high-demand decade of the 1980s. Ideally, then, the United States commands most of the ingredients for a unilateral foreign agricultural policy motored by capacities to reward partners who support our goals and to penalize detractors, much as was done during the 1950s and 1960s.

But the ingredient missing is *legitimacy*. The success of United States policies, including our food policies, in the decades after World War II followed in part from our command of and ability to allocated resources, that is, from our power, so to speak. But it also followed in part from widespread international acceptance of the legitimacy of our pursuits and equally widespread perceptions that American goals complemented global well-being. Needless to say, these acceptances and perceptions have weakened in the face of Third World suspicions and insecurities, assaults from ideological antagonists, debacles in American behavior, and manifestly diminished self-esteem. The United States can no longer expect others to support our policies or acquiesce in our goals because of their self-evident legitimacy, and we can no longer necessarily expect others' compliance and cooperation in deference to our respectability. Because of this, the effectiveness of American unilateralism has been blunted.

Because international organizations are the primary legitimating agents in contemporary international relations, especially in Third World eyes, their multilateral endorsements are crucially important to the success of U.S. foreign policy, including food policy.

In effect, it is increasingly important that the resolutions, decisions, and recommendations of international organizations coincide with American ideals and preferences. This is not to say that the United States must defer to the whims of international parliamentary majorities. Nor, most emphatically, does it mean that the United States should finance unpromising international schemes or assimilate values alien to our traditions. Quite to the contrary, bringing greater coincidence between American preferences and international organizational outcomes means that United States officials must more effectively influence international institutional processes, through more active, more positive, more creative, and, if necessary, more aggressive and dogged participation. Elements of American power remain available—resources, money, and expertise. The challenge in international food affairs for the 1980s is the need to learn how to use these effectively *within* international organizations to foster cooperative action in preferred directions reinforced by global legitimacy.

U.S. Policy and International Organizations: Recommendations for Action

As noted, in many areas, achieving coincidence between American international food objectives and international organizational programs means keeping the world institutions running on tracks already laid by constructive American leadership during the last two decades. That is, it is in the American interest, and it should be an object of American efforts within international organizations, to bring more support for rural development in the Third World, more attention to small farmers and their needs, more concern with nutrition as a public-policy problem, more food security for deficit countries, more research and information concerning agronomic and marketing predictions and problems, more stability in the international market, and more attention to distortions and abuses of free trade.

The United States should also make efforts to improve the operating efficiency and effectiveness of world food organizations. First, there has been great proliferation in the number of food organizations and programs in recent years. This is the result partly of frustrations at the slow pace and apparent ineffectiveness of some of the older institutions, partly the result of enthusiasm generated at the World Food Conference, and largely the result of various coalitions' attempts to structure arenas that are politically and procedurally biased in preferred directions. Obviously, large, industrialized countries feel more comfortable in small, limited-membership organizations with either weighted voting or consensual decision making, while small Third World countries prefer large parlimentary bodies that decide issues on the basis of majority voting. But the result of institutional proliferation, as noted earlier, has been redundancy and confusion in assignments (for example, at least five major organizations are currently debating the issue of food reserves; nine are concerned with food aid; more than a dozen are involved in rural modernization). But, even more seriously, proliferation has brought about a dispersal of resources, as well as considerable waste on redundant administrative and overhead facilities. Greater efficiency in the use of development, food aid, and research funds could be achieved by streamlining the system of world food organizations and better specifying mandates. (This does not imply proliferating further by creating more umbrella organizations or coordinating boards.) While there are obvious political difficulties for the United States in pursuing world food goals through FAO, it is also the case that this organization is structured and mandated to carry out almost all of the tasks that we might like to assign to international organizations. FAO, moreover, has traditional stature and carries considerable respectability in the eyes of many of its members, the Third World states, in particular. Therefore, it is to be recommended that the United States make efforts to strengthen FAO, to concentrate international programs in food and agriculture within FAO, to encourage membership on the part of the Soviet Union, and to rise again to creative leadership within this organization.

Second, the United States should encourage international food organizations to engage in more frequent, more thorough, and more critical evaluations of their programs, with a view toward improving promising ones and eliminating unpromising ones.[32] For institutional and political reasons, reliable self-evaluation is one of the most difficult tasks for any large bureaucratic organization to accomplish. Biases toward self-praise, circumvention, statistical manipulation and inundation, and political sterilization are pronounced in organizational reporting, and the frequent result is that major problems accumulate unattended until crises occur and resources are wasted. In addition, since the funding and functioning of many world food organizations, particularly FAO, depend upon assessments and subscriptions that must be periodically approved by national governments, continuing support depends upon demonstrations of performance in the form of rich, accurate, and freely flowing information about programs and activities. The United States government, and others as well, should be firm in demanding strict accountability from world food organizations, not in the interest of constraining them, but rather toward the end of strengthening them.

American leadership and effectiveness within international organizations depend in considerable measure upon the reasonableness and coherence of our national positions. Yet, there is constant criticism, both within Washington and from other governments and international officials, that American stances tend frequently to be internally inconsistent, diffuse, ambiguous, and varied from organization to organization.[33] The manifest split in the American delegation to the World Food Conference, for example, is a dramatic and embarrassing case in point. Other examples of apparent inconsistency include the U.S. emphasis on the efficacy of the "free market," frequently underlined in our international organizational stances, set beside our willingness to negotiate multiyear bilateral grain agreements outside of the market, or, American reservations about "commodity agreements," expressed at UNCTAD, set beside our efforts at the IWC to create managed food-grain reserves. There may be some underlying consistency in such behavior, but its outward incoherence is understandably puzzling to those with whom we deal. Since coordination in the making of American food policy was the subject of chapter 4, let it suffice here to reiterate simply that greater efforts must be made to integrate the positions of different U.S. executive agencies that address food issues, and to better coordinate the articulation and the funding of food policies in relations between the executive branch and Congress. We do not underestimate the difficulties in such integration, since Americans are not easily constrained to speak with only one voice in either domestic or foreign affairs. Yet, our capacity to lead in international organizations is unquestionably related to our ability to point in clear, unambiguous directions.

Finally, there is the question of the number and quality of people that the United States contributes to the international civil service. Among criticisms of United States effectiveness in FAO, for example, are complaints that there are too few Americans in the FAO secretariat, that some of our nationals working there are distinctly less competent than might be desired, that incentives for younger American officers to enter the international civil service are absent or comparatively unappealing, and that senior technical experts of high competence cannot be recruited for overseas assignments because alternative opportunities in the United States are invariably more attractive to them.[34] The result of this combination of factors is declining American professional influence within international food organizations, and increasing dominance of leadership positions by non-Americans. In light of this, and in view of our recommendation that the United States give greater weight to international organizatioins in its food diplomacy, we urge: (1) that the United States government move rapidly to fill currently vacant positions allotted to our nationals; (2) that it move to expand opportunities for Americans in international civil services, at least to degrees commensurate with our budgetary contributions; (3) that it devise incentives for young officers to improve comparative attractiveness of international as opposed to national service; (4) that it support the upward mobility of competent Americans within international civil services; and (5) that it improve the attractiveness of international assignments for senior experts by providing income or other incentives. Competent people have traditionally been one of America's most valuable foreign-policy resources. Every effort should be made to make optimum use of these resources in the interest of international organizational effectiveness, and in the service of American international food policies.

CHAPTER 6

The Framework for Future United States Policy: Assessing Alternative Risks

Predicting the future is difficult, to say the least. Nevertheless, explicitly, or implicitly, every general policy measure taken by the United States and by other governments affecting the world's system of food production, distribution, and consumption relies upon the prediction of expected results. The basis of policy is either to improve a current situation where this is considered possible, or to ward off some potential future disorder through steps to reduce its likelihood.

In shaping U.S. policy under conditions of increasing global food interdependence, with continuing concern that rising food demand may have very serious negative effects in the foreseeable future, policy makers must foresee the important implications of their decisions. The problems facing American policy makers were outlined in chapter 1. We seek in this chapter to offer a perspective on how policy makers might think about the options they face, and on the risks presented by alternative courses of action.

Alternative Future Outcomes

In the simplest form, possible outcomes over the next decade in world food affairs can be roughly summarized by three scenarios or developmental constructs of the future: (1) the current pattern extended; (2) crisis and disaster; and (3) surprise bounty.[1] These three are sketched below in the rough order that experts' analyses seem to accord them likelihood.

Current Pattern Scenario

Assuming that substantial efforts to increase production in less-developed countries continue to meet with moderate success and that no serious climate or other natural factors intervene, it seems reasonable to expect that an expansion of production will occur throughout the world to meet the growing effective demand, especially of the more affluent peoples of the world. Trade expansion and the dominance of North American grain exports would continue. Population growth, particularly among poor, least-nourished peoples, would offset some gains in nutrition and production, so that the portion of the world's population malnourished in 1985 or 1990 would look much the same as it did in 1965, or in 1974 when Henry Kissinger proclaimed the goal of no child going to bed hungry by 1985.[2]

The problems discussed in chapters 2 and 3 in the commercial and concessional food-trading systems would continue. Prospects of instability and uncertainty would remain objects of concern. Moreover, in this projection, a repetition of the difficulties faced during the 1972–75 period is to be expected sometime in the next decade.[3]

There is a danger that some may interpret such a period benignly, and hence face with equanimity the prospect of a return to shortages. Proponents of "food power" suggest that shortages may supply the United States with a potent weapon in world politics, allowing America to regain the influential position in world affairs that has eroded in the post-Vietnam era. They may be right, but usually they have wrong-headed and probably counter-productive tactics in mind. The United States has successfully squandered food influence on trivial issues, as in forcing Bangladesh to end sales of jute to Cuba in 1974 in return for food aid. We have similarly used food to wring textile-trade restraints from the Koreans and to punish the Jamaicans for raising bauxite prices. Perhaps on a few important issues, such as the Middle East peace, food aid has been used reasonably to cement political arrangements.

For larger political purposes or over a longer time-span, however, purely diplomatic food-power uses are, at best, foolish. To use food as a weapon against the Organization of Petroleum Exporting Countries (OPEC), for instance, would entail much greater risks for us than those which Saudi Arabia would face in using oil as a weapon. Granted that American food exports to OPEC countries have increased dramatically—over tenfold to Saudi Arabia—this food trade is not strictly analogous to oil trade. The United States has a much broader role in world affairs at stake. In addition, the situation in food is quite different from that in oil. Few countries are really vulnerable to food pressures; nearly all are 90 to 95 percent self-sufficient in food. (Japan, which imports about half its food needs, is the notable exception but using "food power" against an important American ally is surely unwise.) In contrast, Europe and Japan must import nearly all their oil, and the United States currently imports half its oil needs. Another factor is that farmers cannot forego the export earnings of food as easily as oil sheiks can take similar losses. In any case, the availability of alternative supplies from other sources makes an effective food embargo practically impossible, as well as morally repugnant. Further, if large American surpluses accumulated, as they can under current conditions of food-supply management, the United States could find the food weapon, if it were used, turned against it by customers.

These limitations on our ability to use food as a weapon will certainly remain, except during the initial periods of a serious shortage. These, of course, may well develop in the next few years, either as a reasonable variation of the current situation (the first scenario), or as a beginning stage of chronic shortages. At that time, what diplomatic concessions could the really vulnerable poor countries of South Asia and Africa offer the United States that would be important enough to risk the opprobrium of denying food to people facing malnutrition and starvation? Many of these countries lack the capacity to manage their own internal affairs with order and coherence. To deny them food aid, even to link it to unacceptable social improvements, would be to risk adding to the hunger, poverty, and degradation of thousands or millions of rural poor. Even the toughest "realist" would find such risks imprudent, and most would agree this was a morally repugnant policy.

Food can be a resource for U.S. diplomacy, but to realize its potential, policy makers should emphasize thinking about food not in bilateral bargains but in a global context. Export discipline, including guarantees for aid during periods of shortage to those making the most concerted efforts to foster their own development, will be an effective way to exercise U.S. responsibility for food. During non-shortage periods, food interdependence can also yield beneficial influence, however diffuse. For instance, it is not necessary to tell Japan that substantial American acreage is devoted to feeding Japanese (more acres in fact than are totally planted in Japan!). This fact is inescapable to Japanese leaders as they make foreign-policy calculations. By not using food power bluntly, and by creating guarantees of reliable supply, we can further foster such interdependence and encourage the general international cooperation that accompanies productive food-exchange relationships.

Recall that this discussion of food used in the "current pattern projected" scenario assumes that gains in agricultural productivity in less-developed countries will occur in response to increased efforts currently under way, so that shortfalls will be less than predicted by the International Food Policy Research Institute. It expects that the level of vulnerability among countries will be roughly equivalent to that of 1972, in spite of improvements in storage and a general growth in the size of the "pipeline" stocks maintained by governments, traders, and farmers. On the other hand, this first scenario does not project indicators warning of dramatically worse times.

Crisis and Disaster

The second scenario does. We have labelled it "crisis and disaster." Here envisage less a Malthusian world of pestilence and war than simply a severe period of chronic shortages. Such a picture has been promoted by a variety of authors, such as Lester Brown, Erik Eckholm, and Georg Borgstrom.[4] This forecast includes two major features: (1) a continued, relative and in some cases absolute, impoverishment of the poor, especially rural poor in the Third World; and (2) the failure of national and international policies to expand production capability and the size of stocks and reserves sufficiently to meet growing effective demand. In this situation, chronic malnutrition would increase dramatically during any production shortfall of the size experienced in 1972 and 1974, while inflation from rising food prices would, or at least could, reach high and uncontrollable levels with a doubling, quadrupling, or more of grain prices at the international level. In this situation the choices might be far more stark for the United States than faced in 1973–74. Should limited supplies of food be shipped abroad to fulfill explicit, or perhaps implicit, commitments to major trading partners, including Europe, Japan, and the Soviet Union, or should it be sent to hard-pressed friendly governments to ward off urban rioting and perhaps the overthrow of governments, especially in Africa and Asia? At what point would domestic political pressures force export controls? And, assuming some need for maintaining exports, how would a national policy of rationing be reached? Government intervention in the United States and elsewhere into agricultural practices and food pricing would dramatically escalate, and the politics of food and agriculture would everywhere be harder and more blatantly engaged. Efforts to impose price ceilings would not only be resented by farmers but would encourage evasion and hoarding and black-market activities on a widespread basis. Even the United States, once it adopted export controls and price policies to hold down domestic inflation, would find political support and legitimacy in the eyes of the farm community eroded.[5]

Internationally, one might expect the United States' capacity for influence to expand dramatically, based on control over scarce food resources. Certainly, one would expect substantial attention to be focused on the United States by foreign governments and peoples, since the United States, along with Canada and a few others, would command sufficient resources to meet at least any single country's national needs. But the United States could not deliver because physical and political-economic limits would intervene. Adjustments would, of course, occur. Export controls would abound; efforts by the most desperate countries would include compelling food stocks held by farmers to be quickly discharged—if necessary, by force of edict or gun. Efforts to avert famine would overwhelm current capabilities for famine relief. Under crisis conditions, wasteful and inadequate welfare operations would be likely; as crop shortages persisted, chronic world welfare programs and continuing dislocation of social order would bring a diminishing of human respect and productivity, and the deterioration of other values.

Within the United States, food issues would not only be politicized at the highest levels, but imposing the "burden of adjustment" would turn into a series of hard decisions. Competing interests in the executive branch would develop entrenched antagonisms on issue after issue, and the efforts in Congress to address the problem and to place the blame for deteriorating food situations in this country and abroad on inadequate foresight and/or current policy compromises in the executive branch would add to the erosion of trust in government. The burden on the executive branch to testify, prepare reports, and otherwise meet congressional efforts to assess the blame would increase substantially.

How long-lasting, and how disruptive, pressures for protection would be, and what reallocation of basic resources into food production (with the subsequent inefficiencies and loss in the production of other goods) would ensue are matters of speculation. The point we wish to make is that such a depressing scenario is widely held to be possible, and has been forecast in varying degrees by respectable studies.[6]

Surprise Bounty

The third scenario we project is one of general abundance. Peasants have been shown to respond quickly to new techniques under conditions of moderate risk and adequate instruction or dem-

Grain Area (million hectares)

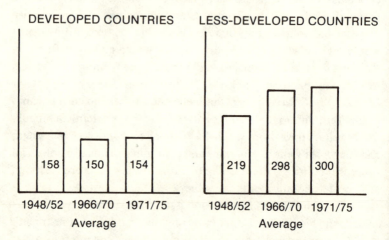

Grain Yields (metric tons per hectare)

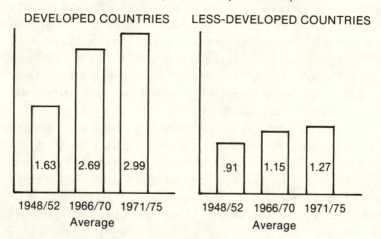

SOURCE: United States Department of Agriculture

Figure 6.1
Expanding Production and Productivity in Developed and Less Developed Countries, 1948–75

onstration. The forecast of increasing demands, increasing emphasis on small-farmer agriculture with its higher per acre yields, and the latent capability, as indicated in figure 6.1, for the expansion of productivity in less-developed countries, could harbinger a world in which production gains are adequate to meet increasing demand and, indeed, to provide modest income gains while holding food prices low. Such a situation, accompanied by economic policies to maintain stable prices and thus protect returns to farmers, as well as by distribution policies that assured food access to the currently malnourished populations of the world, would approximate the lofty goals established at the 1974 World Food Conference.

Not unlike the period of acute shortage, government intervention would be needed when per capita production gains exceeded per capita consumption growth. Surpluses would have to be targeted for nutrition purposes, especially to the young and mothers among the poor populations, thus raising effective demand and food use. Government policies would be needed to regulate surpluses through storage programs. Farm income and continuing production would have to be administratively assured. The bases for such policies exist already in most developed industrialized countries, but are frequently lacking—or often work with perverse and biased effects (as with marketing and price-stabilization boards)—in the developing countries.[7] The result is often that a period of boom is likely to be followed by a period of bust, as experienced in the large swings in the United States prior to the 1930s. Falling food costs in developed countries (relative to other commodities) should have a positive effect on disposable income and general economic growth; moreover, since the farm population of such countries is usually only 3 to 10 percent of the population, policies to protect farm income levels should not be difficult to finance, nor should they be difficult to administer, since substantial experience in doing this already exists. Economic assistance and moderated trade competition would be necessary to assist less-developed surplus countries in managing their problems.

Such a period of supply abundance would also lead to highly

visible budget costs to pay for the necessary management functions of government programs, but the substantial benefits possible in improving health and personal well-being—benefits accruing indirectly most heavily to less-developed countries and poorest peoples—would, we believe, be of inordinate value, and in the long run redound to the general advantage of all countries—notably to industrialized countries in terms of expanded market opportunities and more stable neighbors in an interdependent world. Abundance would be a short-lived phenomenon, at best, unless the costs of managing and sustaining it were met in ways that encouraged increased productivity in all sectors and the use of abundant food supplies to maximize human resource development. Policies to assure this response to surpluses are not high priority at present, a point we return to shortly.

Abundance would also make the programs necessary to attack the debilitating effects of malnutrition less costly and more likely to receive political support from publics which see advantages to concessional domestic food flows. If nutrition programs in less-developed countries were achieved, far-reaching effects in treating the physical and institutional capabilities for better global backup protection against future shortfalls would be derived, especially for those most vulnerable in today's world. Moreover, such an outcome would induce greater respect for the importance of nutrition and the right of people to adequate food, an attitude change that often follows from behavioral change, rather than preceding it. That such redistribution programs are possible is evidenced by the accomplishments of the Chinese, who have not had particularly great success in expanding food production but have achieved heightened quality of life in terms of infant mortality and life expectancy. A recent National Academy of Sciences study, for example, concludes that success in nutrition programs seems to be associated with the fact that countries such as China, Sri Lanka, and a few others "have treated nutrition—calories, protein and other nutrient intake—as only one aspect of the much broader assault on the problem of the very poor." In these countries,

Table 6.1   Quality-of-Life Achievements of Selected
Countries, Early 1970s

	Population (millions) mid-1975	Per capita GNP, 1973 (in 1973 U.S. $)	Life Expectancy at birth (years) 1970-75 average	Death rate per 1,000 population 1970-75 average	Infant mortality per 1,000 live births	Birthrate per 1,000 population 1970-75 average	Literacy rate, 1973	Average daily per capita Caloric Consumption (1969/71)
China	822.8	270	62	10.3	55	26.9	25	2,170
India	613.2	120	50	15.7	139	39.9	34	2,070
Sri Lanka	14.0	120	68	6.4	45	28.6	76	2,170
United States	213.9	6,200	71	9.4	18	16.2	98	3,330

SOURCE: Most data taken or derived from Overseas Development Council, *The U.S. and World Development: Agenda for Action 1976* (New York, 1976), Appendix A-7. Caloric data are from United Nations World Food Conference, *Assessment of the World Food Situation Present and Future* (Rome, November 1974), pp. 51–54.

nutrition programs are embedded in general programs of local development. The data reported in table 6.1 show that China and Sri Lanka have impressive quality-of-life achievements compared to India, although all three have low per capita incomes and low average calories available per capita. Thus, the last of the five problems discussed in chapter 1, malnutrition, is also addressed by the political and economic forces encouraged by supply abundance.

Risk Reduction as an Approach

The worst (and best) outcomes of production growth based on recent trends, on lower than trend growth, and on accelerated growth, are as difficult to assess as the probability of nuclear war, especially a war begun with a surprise attack. Nevertheless, the United States, and many other industrialized countries, regularly invest billions of dollars to reduce the risk of such a nuclear holocaust and to reduce incentives against surprise attack. In less dramatic fashion, other important values of individuals and groups—housing and health, for example—have regularly been the subject of efforts by individuals and societies to insure their preservation, or, should they be destroyed, to prepare practices or strategies that would assure their renewal or restoration, without having the entire burden of such restoration borne directly by those who suffered the loss. Such efforts are commonly called insurance.

The Insurance Concept

Insurance in the form of mutual community obligations dates back to earliest human history, but institutionalized practices among groups with no direct personal relationships is a fairly recent innovation. Even though the risk that a house may be destroyed or a key official in an organization suddenly be lost is low under normal circumstances, the serious effects of such an event induce individuals and organizations to take out insurance to hedge against such loss. In truly "rational" terms, once an insurance system is available, the question faced by individual participants is whether they would prefer to face an unknown but improbable risk of a very large loss or accept paying certain, but low-cost premiums for protection or damage restitution whether a disaster occurs or not.

We recommend this "risk reduction through insurance" approach to thinking about world food problems. There is a range of goals which the United States sensibly seeks in the current context of supply variability, uncertainty about reserve cost sharing and size, and increased, but not yet proven adequate, efforts to expand production in less-developed countries. Pursuing these involves planning for, and responding to, long-run developments in the international food system, including developments thought neither immediately likely nor certain in the longer time frame, but which nonetheless threaten severe damage to a wide range of goals sought by the United States. While these goals interrelate and overlap, as will be clear in chapter 7, an important general element running through all of them is the effort to avert the worst cases in all three scenarios through aggressive government programs to expand worldwide production, improve coordination among commercial exporters and importers, and invigorate the modernization of agriculture through a variety of programs, including concessional food flows, technical assistance, better and more fruitful information, and expanded research efforts. A major assumption behind these goals is that surpluses are better than shortages and that instability (beyond some limits) is undesirable. To avoid this, recommendations to improve government management capabilities, both nationally and internationally, as discussed earlier, need to accompany the efforts suggested in chapter 2 and chapter 3 to reduce instability and expand supply.

These efforts to hedge against the risk entailed in the three broad models of the future seem compelling objectives to us. This is because if the worst outcomes in each case occur, either through failures of nature or policy, we will be prepared to limit the damage and restore losses where possible. Even in the best scenario, with surpluses in excess, the cost of "overcorrecting" against the contingency of shortages will be far less than the benefits derived from the surplus. The insurance principle suggests not only hedging against risks, but also spreading the costs of the collective good derived from insurance. It further suggests minimizing the extent to which insurance is called upon by reducing the vulnerability to loss of those participating in world food markets and concessional systems. This entails, as we discuss later, emphasis on rural development and the establishment of self-reliance and mutual guarantees that manage and stabilize the food exchange of the world.

Insurance against the Worst
in Each Scenario

Since each of the three scenarios has some bad features, it makes sense to take out insurance against these in all three cases. In chapter 7 we outline policy goals aimed to do this. There are, of course, inevitable trade-offs between policies and collective assurance efforts, national and international, aimed at alleviating the worst in one situation and that in another. We emphasize avoiding the worst of the worst case, chronic shortages, but recognize the need for balancing among competing risks to be reduced.

Consider the worst case that we wish to insure against. In a stiuation where supply chronically falls short of expanding demand, we can expect severe consequences as outlined earlier, including dramatic and unavoidable losses in human resources, especially among younger children and babies, for whom the losses will be irreversible and for whom both short- and long-term expenses for health, emergency relief, and welfare may place yet further burdens both on poor-country governments and on the United States and international welfare efforts in general.

Even the more moderate shortage case, the current situation projected, contains elements of the "worst." Recall that even when supply on average keeps up with effective demand, lack of policy protection and climatic uncertainty remain. Substantial fluctuations in production in individual countries are therefore likely, as evidenced by a drop of 80 million tons in Soviet production experienced in 1975, and while these shortfalls tend to be dispersed around the world in such a way as to smooth supply instability, there are still destabilizing swings ranging between 1 percent and 4 percent from trend.[8] Without greater national and international efforts to stabilize production and to raise it above current levels of growth in less-developed countries, this current situation projected contains a number of bad tidings. First, uncertainty will remain high as the food system as a whole remains vulnerable to the impact and costs of global moderate shortages. Second, vulnerability will be even higher and more costly for the rural poor and the chronic malnourished with little or no backup guarantees on their access to food. A third feature in this scenario will be the drag on economic growth resulting from the side effects of malnutrition and from the unrealized productive potential of agriculture in less-developed countries. Fourth, in the United States (and in other industrialized producing countries), significant price fluctuations will continue to reinforce farmer and industry expectations of potential high profits. Even if a strictly economic analysis might show that average farm income price fluctuations would be identical to that under a smoother, government-managed price system, with large fluctuations farmers will in fact expect their incomes to be higher, and political protest is likely therefore to be substantial at each downturn. In addition, the intermittent price rises are likely to have a ratcheting effect on the overall economy, driving inflation further upward than otherwise. In the United States, for instance, food costs were a driving force in inflation during 1978 and 1979. Finally, under the current (1979) system, with no government or international reserves and few international guarantees, we expect the United States would be less able to use food as a resource to achieve international objectives. In particular, the capacity to be consistent and reliable in providing aid for development, in supplying food for export trade, and in making predictable contributions to balance of payments is jeopardized.

What happens in the case of an acceleration of per capita food yields in the world? Since the 1950s, developed country per capita food production has grown about 30 percent; in the less-developed countries it has grown nearly 10 percent, despite their high population growth rates (although distribution is quite uneven and a good many countries have experienced per capita decreases). These increases have been absorbed by growing demand. Still, even higher production growth could outstrip demand. Such an outcome, thanks to the fortuitous combination of technological diffusion, generally favorable weather and climate conditions, and lower cost and/or more efficient combination of production inputs, would, of course, alleviate many of the bad outcomes expected in our first two scenarios. Yet, even in this case, increased national and international coordination to manage food policy and assure equitably distributed gains from growing productivity is needed. Otherwise, even this best case will have some bad outcomes. Among these will be the struggle to maintain farm income as food prices fall relative to other goods. This will involve direct government costs, necessarily financed by taxpayers in programs that compete with defense and welfare programs already in existence in most countries. A second problem posed by this best case would be increased pressure in major exporting countries to dump surpluses on world markets. This would likely generate increased demands on government officials to bargain out arrangements among exporters. It would be desirable if excess food resources could be absorbed in expanded food and nutrition programs, ones particularly aimed at humanitarian development goals. At some point, of course, expanding production could lead to excesses beyond what current and future storage facilities can handle, and rotting and waste would dramatically increase. Furthermore, without income supports, an economic recession could substantially damage farm areas. To the extent that other sectors of the economy could not absorb the decreasingly profitable farm labor and input, farm depression could trigger a more general economic difficulty. Government storage and income support programs, however, once the subject of scornful criticism, may have avoided such an outcome in the United States in the 1950s and the 1960s, when surplus stocks relative to consumption were on occasion three or more times higher than in 1978.[9]

Conclusion

There are many who think that increased food production, especially in less-developed countries, will solve the problems of interdependence. Such increased production, produced by whatever mix of expanding farm inputs and improving technology, is certainly possible. But, in itself, it provides no complete solution to the most serious and chronic problems identified in chapter 1. Malnutrition, income instability, and poverty can at best be only marginally alleviated by higher crop yields. As we have tried to argue above, most of the bad things that make food production, distribution, and consumption a matter of global concern are beyond the reach of scientific and technical solutions. Indeed, we suspect that the more exotic "solutions" to food problems, such as capital intensive production of new proteins, probably pose even more serious problems[10] because of their likely high price and low labor component. Simply comparing the gap in production yields between developed and less-developed countries as shown in figure 6.1 strongly suggests there is room for dramatic improvement in crop yields even without dramatic new technologies.[11]

In general, then, we do not forecast chronic and universal food shortages in the future, because the world's ability to adjust to increasing food demand and to absorb geographically dispersed crop failures is promising, given existing levels of technology and global transfer capacity. Still, local, regional, and intermittent food shortages are likely in the years ahead, and the real problem seems to be how to manage adjustments to cope with these in ways that hedge against turning shortages into "crises" and crises into "panics."

In the past, the United States has borne a major portion of the burden of world adjustment to changing food and agricultural conditions. It remains true that this country is still endowed with some of the best farmland in the world; some of it is still available for expanded production. Further, the American technological base in agriculture is the most advanced in the world. With such natural and technological resources at our disposal, a failure to use them aggressively to address food problems arising in an interdependent world is likely to result in lost opportunities for the United States to fulfill important goals. Such a lack of leadership would also be a failure for human progress more generally.

What choices does the United States face in looking at the framework for its future policy? As we have underlined, all scenarios turn up policy problems for the United States. Can this country, as it did to a large extent in the 1950s and 1960s, exercise leadership and execute global adjustment on its own? Our judgment is that the possibilities for going it alone in attempting to regulate world grain adjustments, with minimum cost-sharing and mutuality among participants in the global food system, are slim. Domestic political and economic forces, unleashed by inflation, declining real incomes, and the decreasing political importance of farmers will prohibit such policies in the future. Furthermore, international opinion would resent "imperial" policies, and others' actions could easily frustrate them. Moreover, there is no reason why the United States should unilaterally assume responsibility for the collective good of mankind.[12]

What, then, is to be said of a policy of encouraging a thoroughly decentralized response to food problems of the future—that is, let each government be responsible for its own citizens, and let national self-sufficiency in food be the universal standard? From all that we have said thus far, we obviously do not advocate this formula either. Clearly, there is a great deal to be said for encouraging every country to achieve the highest economically efficient levels of food production, given its resources. But, this would not result in dramatically reducing the current level of food interdependence. There is at least one reason why reducing global food interdependence would be difficult and undesirable for the United States. This is the fact that food interdependence is part of a broader pattern of interdependence in the global political economy, and American stakes in nurturing this pattern are high. The cost of every country's seeking food security through self-sufficiency would be reduced efficiency in world production, decline in trade volumes, and lessened demand (and work) for suppliers and receivers, shippers, market managers, and all whose livelihoods and responsibilities are linked to international transfers. Economically, world welfare would suffer. In fact, the reverberating effects of such autarchic efforts in food might inspire world recession or depression. Politically, the groups disadvantaged most also happen to be among the strongest supporters of globalism, international harmony, and conflict control, and their support for peaceful international affairs would be weakened. Moreover, reducing interdependence would also mean eliminating the capacity of any country to rely on others for backups or reserves in the event that policies of self-sufficiency fail. It is true, as Richard Cooper points out, that the effect of interdependence has been to reduce governments' abilities to achieve national objectives.[13] But, interdependence has grown nonetheless, because national policy makers have found in it enhanced opportunities for achieving national goals through cooperative activities among states. Since interdependence has grown as the gains from it have perceptibly outweighed losses, is there any reason to believe that the reverse of this will hold true in the future? We think not, particularly for food, and especially if interdependence can be guided to mature into cost as well as benefit sharing.

To spread food production more heavily into areas where marginal land will be brought into production will likely increase the total variability in world production and hence exacerbate one of the primary maladies of the present system.[14] This, in turn, would have an adverse effect on importers among industrialized countries who count upon predictable supplies, and more dramatically upon certain less-developed countries that the United States now seeks to assist economically. The effort to escape from interdependence is likely therefore to postpone and perhaps outrightly frustrate steps necessary to overcome food problems specifically and development problems more generally. Moreover, not only might reducing interdependence make global economic problems worse, but by encouraging such a retreat from interlinkedness the United States would be reducing the value of one of the few resources in which is has special advantage. Overall, the record of some countries' attempts to enhance national well-being through uneconomic programs of import substitution was a near disaster with regard to industrial goods in the 1950s and 1960s. There is no reason to believe that the case with food would be different in the 1980s and 1990s.

The compelling direction for U.S. policy, given this future framework, is to pursue an expansion of the global capacity for intergovernmental cooperation. Nurturing interdependence by sharing the burden of providing food security, by realizing understandings on reserves for purposes of price stability and reliability in food, and through sharing the obligations to alleviate malnutrition by attacking poverty, is an important goal. It should be institutionalized in international life. But the traps of interdependence must be avoided. Going it alone, and avoiding responsibility by preaching self-reliance, are dysfunctional options, for the United States as well as for others. Equally damaging would be "free riding" on others' efforts to maintain order and bring well-being, and any country's attempt to do this should be frustrated.[15] The success of United States efforts to use food resources to buttress interdependence could substantially determine the nature and severity of the next shortage situation, and thereby crucially affect whether the race between food supply and ever-growing demand continues to be won.

CHAPTER 7

Global Food Interdependence and the Challenge to American Policy

Reviewing United States foreign argicultural policy in light of global food problems leads to the conclusion that America's international behavior has neither been totally callous nor completely virtuous. Since World War II, American policy actions have furthered interdependence in the global food system by fostering lower trade barriers, expanding food trade through concessional sales, encouraging greater reliance on imported higher-technology production inputs, enhancing food security for food importers, and alleviating hardships during disasters. In addition, American leadership has contributed to degrees of cooperation, coordination, and organization in global food affairs that are rather extraordinary in a politically fragmented world. On balance these developments were benign.

Unfortunately, since 1972, the performance of the international food system, and to a lesser extent the contribution of the United States, can be seriously questioned. Price instability, supply uncertainty, rising malnutrition, continuing rural poverty, heightened concern about eventual chronic shortages, and confusion and impasse in international relations are all problems attributable in some measure to failures, oversights, and misplaced priorities in American policy. In its commercial aspects, American foreign agricultural policy has been rather irresponsible since 1973, both in abetting market instabilities and in provoking perceptions of food insecurity. Moreover, U.S. policy has not been particularly attentive to inequities in food distribution between or within countries, and the goal of qualitatively improved diets around the world has largely been paid no more than lip service. American policy has not been very definite in encouraging rural modernization in Third World countries (until very recently), and American leadership in world food organizations, once quite significant, is waning.

Given the importance of food trade for the United States, and the foreign policy advantages to be gained in exploiting our agricultural abundance, a strategy that would reduce the United States' role in international food affairs seems neither wise nor practical. American food interdependence is substantial and unlikely to decline. The question at issue throughout this study, therefore, has been: How can the United States use its food resources to the best advantage? Successive chapters have been variations on the central theme that policies are needed that serve both national and international food goals and that concurrently address other food-related problems, such as the North-South dialogue over the international economic order and the principles of international relations for the 1980s.

The Goals of American Participation in Global Food Affairs

American goals and interests in the orderly evolution of food-related international activities are manifold. We summarize below seven goals particularly discussed in earlier chapters and which should be pursued with vigor. Two frequently cited goals for American food resources are excluded from our list: food power diplomacy and population control.

Food power, as discussed in chapter 6, is a misleading and dangerous way to use America's food abundance when understood as withholding food to secure specific price or diplomatic objectives.

There is no effective way to blackmail either the Soviet Union or Saudi Arabia with threats of denying them access to food. The openness of the world trading system and the alternative supply and adjustment options available to them make narrow food power ideas untenable. The demand for "a barrel of oil for a bushel of wheat" will not work.

Linking access to food or provision of food aid to the willingness of the recipient to undertake population limitation is also a bad idea. Aside from modest AID support for combined health, nutrition and birth control services in rural centers, including some PL480 food, there is little virture in linking food policy to population control. Of course, controlling population growth and achieving some tolerable maximum global populace are critical to an eventual end to malnutrition. It is also critical to other problems arising from growing demand on other limited resources including energy and raw materials. However, the methodology of food production and the bureaucratic regulation of its distribution are distinctive. Food specialists are not population specialists. There may be indirect benefits for population control from more adequate nutrition, as the low birth rate in Kerala following its effective steps to alleviate malnutrition suggests. Let these benefits accure indirectly, however, not through forcing a "coordination" of food and population policy. The seven goals of American policy we recommend, therefore, should serve American interests without intruding upon or abusing other countries or forcing together distinctively separate issues.

1. Maintain and expand markets for food exports. Projections of production to the year 1990 (and beyond) indicate that American agriculture will continue to be capable of producing substantial food surpluses. Similar projections show growing food deficits in other parts of the world, even after considerable progress in agricultural development. Opportunities to market American surpluses abroad therefore will continue to exist, and the United States should take advantage of its resource abundance. Both commercial and concessional exports serve important foreign policy goals through helping other states meet nutritional, humanitarian, and political/economic needs. In addition, American overseas food marketing generates needed foreign exchange in this country, improves farm income directly, and, via multiplier effects, national income and employment. It also facilitates agricultural policies that can be premised upon low costs to American taxpayers and low degrees of government intervention into the workings of markets. (chapter 2)

2. *Manage international food interdependence to the mutual satisfaction of all participants in the market.* Benefits to the United States from international food markets accrue most readily and consistently under conditions of reasonable price stability and security of supply. Contrary conditions, while sometimes promising short-term profits (as in the 1973–74 period) tend to prompt private hoarding, dumping, import or export restrictions, and other ad hoc and perverse behaviors that redound to damage some or all market participants and frequently the market itself. (chapter 2)

3. *Prevent food shortages from undermining the economic development and political stability of Third World countries.* Adequate food and the contribution of progressive agriculture to economic development in the Third World is in the American interest for a host of political, economic, military-strategic, and humanitarian reasons. In its broadest definition, pursuing "American security" means acting to create and maintain an external environment benign to the survival and flourishing of the deepest values of our society. These values are in jeopardy in a politically volatile world of destitute, hungry, and angry people, who are easily roused in their desperation by anti-American ideologies and ideologues. Beyond these rather fundamental interests in political-military stability in Third World countries, the countries' economic development and their integration into the world economy are linked to American prosperity now, and increasingly as we approach the turn of the century. Therefore, to the extent that food scarcities threaten Third World

development, alleviating them remains an American interest and goal. (chapter 3)

4. *Meet emergency acute scarcity situations decisively, efficiently, and adequately.* Famines and near famines occur intermittently throughout the world. In some regions they recur regularly. It is in the American interest both to contribute to international famine-relief efforts and to support and encourage the development of international disaster-relief institutions. Humanitarianism and generosity are traditional elements of American foreign policy. Our self-respect demands that they should continue as such. While there is little evidence that demonstrations of international goodwill are necessarily requited, generosity in famine relief is certainly beneficial to the respect given to America abroad. Beyond countries' generosity, effective famine relief requires efficient organization and administration at the international level. Therefore, out of pragmatic concerns for eliminating waste and confusion in relief operations, and for more principled reasons concerning the importance of international organizations in contemporary world affairs, it is in the interest of the United States to help strengthen the United Nations Disaster Relief Office and related institutions. (chapter 3)

5. *Keep United States participation in global food affairs consonant with the aims and interests of domestic farm, food, and economic policies.* The interests of the agricultural sector illustrate especially well the key problems in global interdependence; that is, the potential for conflict and mutual harm between international and domestic policy pressures and processes. Reasonable income growth for American farmers, strong and stable domestic markets, and orderly structural reform in agriculture are traditional goals of farm policy that demand continual political attention. Equally important are the nutritional well-being of Americans at all income levels and the macroeconomic well-being of the nation. To the extent that global food conditions and marketing practices affect these domestic concerns (and in recent years they have affected them rather dramati-

cally) legislative and administrative steps must be taken to buffer their impacts. On the other hand, foreign-policy goals connected with American export capacities in both commercial and concessional dealings are sufficiently important that they cannot be abandoned each time domestic goals, such as holding down inflation, fall into jeopardy. High priority among American goals therefore should be accorded to structuring and executing policy-making activities that are open and responsive to (but not controlled by) diverse food and agricultural interests, and that orchestrate these into multifaceted, but logically and politically consistent, courses of action. (chapter 4)

6. *Strengthen, rationalize, and legitimize United States objectives in global food affairs within the system of international organizations.* Accomplishing most American goals in food and agriculture (domestic and international) requires regular, orderly, and continuing communication with other governments. It also requires soliciting others' wisdom and eliciting their cooperation. Further, it necessitates accumulating and disseminating information, amassing and investing capital, and, of course, distributing food. These activities tend to occur today in an international political-economic setting where the great majority of governments prefer to conduct their diplomacy within multilateral institutions. Ignoring these institutions, undervaluing their significance, and retreating from them can only frustrate American goals. On the other hand, the interest of the United States and its international aims in food and agriculture are better served by efforts to make international organizations more receptive to American leadership, to make their programs more reflective of American policies and preferences, and to make their management more rational. (chapter 5)

7. *Plan for and respond to likely longer-run developments in the international food system.* Conventional policy-making and administration, informed by short-run analysis and geared to immediate objectives, will prove inadequate (and perhaps extremely harmful) in response to evolving supply and demand conditions in the global food system. Foreign food and agricultural policy must protect pro-

ducers and consumers both against disruptive cyclical shifts in weather and marketing conditions, and against rather ominous secular movements linked to resource exhaustion, expanding population, economic growth (and possible climatic change). The unpredictability of the future was stressed in chapter 1. Complex interrelationships among the social, economic, and technological factors that will generate the food situation of the 1980s and 1990s are not well understood. Nonetheless, it should be a goal of American policy to insure against "worst case" eventualities, both for this country and for the world more generally, and to gain maximum advantage for any more favorable outcomes that might materialize. Under no circumstances must short-run expendiencies be permitted to raise the probabilities of future disaster. (chapter 6)

The United States and the Global Food System: Some Recommended Courses of Action

The review and analysis in our previous chapters provide the bases for our policy goals. Numerous specific recommendations for action have already been mentioned and these can be summarized under five prevailing prescriptive themes:

1. Greater stability in international food marketing should be guaranteed through policies, agreements, and institutionalized facilities that create orderly marketing arrangements and a system of grain reserves.

2. Rural modernization in poor countries should be promoted with increased vigor.

3. The United States governmental organization for coordinating domestic and international policy should be further integrated and revised to allow for the more effective delegation of policy-implementing decisions.

4. Multilateral agencies should be accorded more support and use.

5. Several specific research efforts should be undertaken: to

estimate the extent and cost of malnutrition; to explore the costs and benefits of alternative food-production technologies in various settings; and to search for resources, procedures, and means of change to achieve the major goals of market stability and rural modernization. Research applied to specific problems of food and agriculture should follow from theoretical development in the natural and social sciences.[1]

Market Stability

Price stability in international food markets was guaranteed shortly after World War II, and until 1972, by massive government-held food reserves and by the reserve production capacity of major exporters and large producers. United States reserves, in particular, provided stability and security through "redundancy." This stability was based on the key role of grains as a food source that could be easily substituted for other foods, could be stored for several years, and could be relied upon to be in surplus because the domestic farm program in the United States was politically important and had the effect of stimulating a large supply that the government had to stockpile in order to maintain floor prices. During the late 1960s and early 1970s, changes in United States agricultural policy (paralleled by changes in Canada and Australia) allowed this reserve to disappear. When demand rose substantially in 1972–73 because of unexpected purchases by the Soviet Union, bad crops due to adverse weather in a number of countries, and declining availabilities of food products, such as the Peruvian anchovy, major price instability occurred. The "costs" of this instability are hard to calculate; at a minimum the tripling of wheat prices during the perceived "crisis" period of 1973–74, ruined economic planning and balance-of-payment calculations in a large number of less-developed food-importing countries. Inflation was fueled globally. Political discontent and erratic economic performances were manifested in countries such as the United States that bore the adjustment costs directly, and the attention of political and bureaucratic elites shifted to the food problem. The obvious solution, an international reserve in which those who benefit from reasonable price stability and food security share the costs, was agreed to at the 1974 World Food Conference. After five years of subsequent discussions it has not been achieved. We recommend that the United States should continue to press for a global food reserve, accumulated and regulated by an international authority or by a system of national commitments under a multilateral agreement. Yet, taking account of obstacles currently in the way of a global reserve agreement, and bearing in mind that the absence of a reserve invites another crisis reminiscent of 1973–74, we further recommend that the United States establish unilaterally an emergency reserve targeted for poor-country concessional needs and develop further reserve policies that would guarantee commercial stability and security by working on its own or in collaboration with a few other major exporters. Such "independent national means" solutions should provide incentives to importers—both rich and poor— to collaborate to insure their future supplies. Furthermore, the international purpose for this reserve, and the structure of agreements and commitments between exporters and importers that define and constrain its use, should guarantee that the reserve would not function primarily to satisfy domestic farm pressures. The latter characterized the previous United States reserve experience and was a disincentive for collaboration by importers. The United States, or United States-Canadian-Australian collective-security reserve systems could provide priority access to LDCs and to those who pay a share of the costs of maintaining the reserve.

Beyond proposing a reserve as the key element in guaranteeing stability and security, we recommend that a number of additional steps should be taken (or reaffirmed) to guarantee orderly marketing. For one thing, erratic and massive interventions and withdrawals from the international market as perpetrated by the Soviet Union in 1972 should be militated against. When entered into cautiously, with due concern for the dangers in artificially constraining supply and demand, long-term supply agreements such as those concluded with the Russians in 1975 are appropriate, as are procedures for monitoring large grain sales established after the disruptive Russian interventions. Ultimately, however, the Soviet Union ought to be pressed to provide more information about its crop conditions and food-import policies, so that the international market might better adjust in a timely manner to intermittent Soviet needs without penalizing either Russian or non-Russian consumers. Second, the United States should resist perpetrating erratic jarrings of the international food market on its own part. The impact of our embargo of soybean exports in 1973, especially in Japan, albeit negligible economically, was psychologically damaging. Confidence both in the United States as a food supplier and in the world trading system as a buttress to food security was undermined. Third, pressures for the liberalization of trade in foodstuffs should be continued, especially given the limited progress in this area at the Multilateral Trade Negotiations of 1976–79. Nevertheless, relations with the European Economic Community in the realm of agriculture might better focus upon possible liberalizations and reciprocities at the margin (in cheese and other dairy products, for example) than upon grand differences of philosophy about agricultural policy. Over the longer run, the Common Agricultural Policy of the EC is likely to evolve under internal pressures toward greater premium on efficiency and greater respect for an international division of labor. Until then, American "assaults on the C.A.P." as discussed in chapter 2 are likely to generate only ill will between policy elites who should be occupied with more pressing transatlantic problems.

Rural Modernization

Raising food production in Third World countries is the primary means of preventing food shortages, and as such, is an essential element in economic development. Since there is a sharp limit on what the United States unilaterally, or the major food exporters collectively, can do ultimately to supply the food needs of all of the expanding populations of the Third World, emphasis in our policy must be placed upon aiding and encouraging others to raise local production. In most countries faced with chronic scarcity, production can only be raised through heightened land and/or labor productivity; that is, through rural modernization. Avenues to launching and sustaining rural modernization are to be found in breaking down constraints on development caused by shortages of capital, shortages of inputs demanded by advanced agronomic technologies, and by inadequate agricultural research, too few and poorly trained agricultural administrators and extension workers, and uneducated, inadequately skilled farmers. Rural transformation and industrialization must be meshed in the Third World; and both can be aided by United States financial assistance, unilaterally or multilaterally channeled, by technical assistance, food aid and research support. Rural modernization poses both a set of technical problems, for example, whether to emphasize export crops or domestic food crops, and political problems, for example, how to attack the social and institutional barriers to the productivity of the rural poor. Although direct American intervention to raise the priority given rural modernization and equitable development is not plausible or recommended, U.S. assistance policies should be consistently geared to reward those countries whose efforts are the greatest in this regard.

Governmental Organization

Domestic and foreign policy objectives concerning American food and agriculture are equally important, and they are complementary under most conditions. Yet the realities of American politics have demonstrated that when domestic goals fall into jeopardy, external goals tend to be abandoned, and costs are incurred with regard to overseas markets, foreign-exchange earnings, and the attitudes of customers and clients. Only by integrating and orchestrating domestic and foreign agriculture and food policies can we avoid the intermittent victimizing of either Americans or foreigners. Since American food policies, domestic and foreign, are important to a variety of interests—producers, traders, economic planners, consumers, diplomats, and humanitarians, it is unreasonable to imagine that tensions and bureaucratic conflicts, such as those that arose in 1973–74, can or should be avoided by reorganizing the many agencies that shape food policy into a new "super" institution or under the authority of one specialized office. The basic problem is to establish clear priorities and points of trade-off among competing interests, and to minimize possible conflicts through policies that make extreme price pressures unlikely. If international objectives are given greater weight, then assured supplies based on food surpluses (reserves) take on added importance. Domestic adjustment policies must be designed to support sales and food-aid policies, and the implementation of foreign policy must be placed in the line agency that has the greatest stake in the policy's success. To facilitate coordination among interests and objectives, interagency institutionalized and ad hoc committees continue to be needed. An interagency working committee for PL 480 should continue, but responsibility for its leadership and program implementation should be placed in the development agency, the United States Agency for International Development, or its successor, since the primary purpose of food aid should be developmental and humanitarian rather than surplus disposal. Such interagency bodies should be able to make decisions and see to their implementation. We see no necessity for coordinating food policy in the White House.

Ad hoc groups, such as the Commission on Domestic and International Hunger and Nutrition, as with earlier task forces and interagency committees, can play an important role in setting priorities and monitoring the various policies and agencies that deal with food. This commission and other bodies should be able to forward for presidential action recommendations on domestic and international policy germane to the basic goals of food security and eliminating hunger. Unfortunately such groups meet too often merely for discussion; their effectiveness is dissipated and the effective American response to hunger becomes largely rhetorical.

International Organization

Since the World Food Conference, the number, complexity and formal responsibilities of international bodies have expanded significantly. The United States, on the whole, has played a supportive role in the formation of the World Food Council (WFC), the International Fund for Agricultural Development (IFAD), and the Consultative Group on International Food Production and Investment (CGFPI). In order to make effective use of these bodies, and to take advantage of the legitimacy accorded multilateral coordination and innovation, the United States should progressively increase its commitments to international institutions and programs, particularly the World Food Program, the International Fund for Agricultural Development, and the Food Aid Convention, where U.S. food-aid commitments should be an exemplar to encourage collaboration in meeting concessionary and commercial grain needs of importing countries. This is the best hope for securing greater food-aid pledges from other OECD countries, from the more prosperous "developing" countries, and from the socialist states. Greater coordination of efforts should be sought through more donor/recipient consortia that emphasize food production and food import goals, as in the Bangladesh consortium. United States cooperation should continue, and indeed increase, in international organizational programs designed to accumulate and disseminate the findings of agronomic research. So, too, should this country cooperate with, and actively lead, in FAO and other international efforts at global crop forecasting, indicative planning, regulating international agribusiness, and providing early warning about emergent adversity. FAO and UNDP rivalry should be reduced, and ways to have bilateral and multilateral foreign assistance programs more coordinated and reinforcing should be sought. The case for cooperation in preparing and administering international disaster relief has been made already. What needs special emphasis in this regard is the need to encourage the governments of disaster-prone areas (for example, Sahelian Africa, monsoon Asia) to hold modest stocks *in advance* and to share these equitably, so as to efficiently and quickly distribute international disaster assistance. Such "encouraging" is best accomplished by financial incentives that arrive under the mantle of legitimacy provided by international organization.

On a more philosophical plane, the diplomacy of food takes place at present in an international political atmosphere charged by tension and suspicion, where *equality, participation,* and *new order* are major demands of poorer countries. While tensions arise largely outside the working domain of food officials, they nevertheless permeate the environment of international dealings. Given the requirements for accomplishing American goals in international food affairs, especially inasmuch as this often implies collaborative or complementary behavior on the part of others, it may well be that only multilateral forums can facilitate essential policy compromises and encourage essential flows of research, finance, and food. If international relations are bound to become more "participatory" in years ahead, as Third World countries become increasingly active, we believe that the United States should lead the way toward "participatory democracy" within the constitutional frameworks of international organizations. This country should surely not pace a retreat toward new anarchy, by devaluing international institutions, and shunning global cooperation.

Research

In recent years, budgets of the Agricultural Research Service, the various centers supported by the Consultative Group in International Agricultural Research (CGIAR), and the Agency for International Development have grown substantially. Title XII legislation has allowed for substantial support to American agricultural schools to encourage research beneficial to international agricultural development. A major portion of these funds, however, has gone to strengthen existing domestic institutions and research initiatives. Some critics believe the funds are largely a trough to feed American academics. Certainly, nearly all the research has a technical and cultural component of Western science. Very little effort has been made to undertake new types of research that could lead to changed government priorities, or to cultural and social changes. In particular, the costs of malnutrition to particular societies in terms of the loss to economic production and additional health services have received little attention. It is possible that economic productivity could be enhanced by improving a population's diet; if so, the priority given to "right to food" principles and nutritional concerns should be increased. Other issues are raised by alternative land tenure and technology policies.

The advantages of competing alternatives should also be studied. Resolving some of the controversy over the desirability of various landholding and capital-input strategies for increasing production is important to assist more informed policy decisions in developing countries and more selective project appraisals by funding agencies. Similarly, research on the institutions that will best serve goals of equitable rural modernization and universal food security is needed. Much remains to be done, for example, toward assessing the efficacies of varieties of rural-ownership institutions. Collectivization may be considered an ideological evil and left at that. Or, its appropriateness or inappropriateness under varying conditions might be thoroughly assessed.[2] Once again, in the same vein, the idea of growing nonfood export crops on the best agricultural land of food-deficit countries, may be dismissed as unwise (and perhaps inhumane).[3] On the other hand, these may be optimum practices for both the countries in question and for the international economy under appropriate conditions. Research is needed to identify such conditions, and a priori political and ideological assumptions can only hinder constructive results. Other possible innovations needing research are long-term commodity arrangements, grain reserves in less-developed countries, developmental uses of food aid, and international crop insurance.

Finally, a good deal of more or less "pure" research in the natural and social sciences is also needed, and much of this can be conducted in the United States where research institutions and expertise abound. In the natural sciences, many of the mysteries of photosynthesis remain to be solved, as do problems of nitrogen fixing, nutrient content in grains, DNA chemistry, and a host of others. For their part, social scientists are theoretically hampered by an as yet primitive understanding of the economics of development, agriculture's role in development, and development in nonmarket economies (i.e., most LDC economies). Similarly, far too little is known about the relationships between political and social institutional change, and economic growth (especially in non-Western systems), and almost nothing (save for anecdotal examples) is known about the political implications of widespread hunger, beyond the fact that these are likely to be severely unstabilizing.

American Leadership and the Principles of Food Diplomacy

Advocating greater American leadership as we have done at various points in our study amounts to a cliché unless it is accompanied by more specific directions. We believe that leadership is as much an attribute of moral authority as it is a correlate of physical capability. Such authority is exerted by basing policies upon enunciated principles that others can recognize and accept as legitimate, appropriate, and rational under existing circumstances. In this sense, American leadership in foreign affairs stems both from our capacity to expend resources on policy objectives, and, equally importantly, from the recognized rectitude of the principles that inform our policies and guide our actions.

Under the Carter administration, the government of the United States has, superficially at least, attempted to fashion a foreign policy based upon principles of elevating "human rights" globally, preserving East-West "détente," and meeting "basic human needs" among the world's poor. All of these principles are controversial both within this country and without but elaborating on this controversy is beside the point that we are driving at. What is important is that foreign-policy officials are once again attempting to articulate exactly what it is that this country stands for and against in global affairs, and that they are equally endeavoring to attract others' adherence to the rectitude of our moral stances.

We endorse this moral thrust in American foreign policy, and we recommend that the United States attempt to exert greater authority in international food affairs by enunciating and emphasizing broad principles that should guide American and other countries' food policies. By way of conclusion, then, let us briefly summarize these principles that we believe the United States ought to stand for, and against, in global food affairs.

1. *Development should be the paramount priority of food diplomacy.* Rural modernization in the Third World is most urgently needed if the global food system is going to stand up to the pressures of the 1980s. American declarations and actions should emphasize this urgency, and underline that Third World development is the collective responsibility of the total community of nations. Behavior encouraging development should be engaged, applauded, and supported by the United States; behavior discouraging it should be condemned.

2. *Nutrition should be a central concern of food diplomacy.* Chronic hunger is an affliction affecting humanity in epidemic proportions. American policy should be founded upon the conviction

that debilitating malnutrition anywhere in the world is intolerable, and that overcoming it is the urgent concern and legitimate responsibility of the community of nations.

3 *Adequate diet is a human right and should be a diplomatic concern.* The injustice and intolerability of vast differences in levels of food consumption between and within countries ought to be a central concern of American policy. American declarations and actions ought, therefore, to make it known that we consider it both wrong and unacceptable that some countries enjoy sumptuous levels of per capita food intake while others teeter at the margin of mass starvation. We further consider it wrong and unacceptable that some national governments tolerate obvious overconsumption by some of their citizens and the simultaneous starvation of others. Monitoring such conditions within countries is a legitimate concern of the international community. Their perpetuation should be internationally condemned.

4. *Food aid is a right and an obligation.* The United States should continue to support the principle which deems concessional food distributions essential, functional, and humane, so long as hunger exists. It is wrong that people should starve because they lack the means to purchase food, and enhancing their welfare is an obligation of all responsible members of the international community. Other purposes of food aid, however, must be subordinated in its allocation; it may not be legitimately used primarily for doling out political rewards, or used to increase food dependency.

5. *Agricultural information should flow freely.* American policy should continue to uphold the principle that agricultural science and technology are collective goods developed for the benefit of mankind. The government should similarly adhere to, and emphasize, the conviction that information about agricultural conditions within any nation must be made available to all nations, since the orderly evolution of markets and development plans depend crucially upon such information.

6. *The stability of food markets should be enhanced.* American policy should be guided by the conviction that the human costs of extreme price fluctuations on international food markets are too high to be written off as unavoidable hardships of supply and demand adjustment. Therefore, while the legitimacy of distribution via the international commercial system must continue to receive strong American support, the principle of "stable markets" should nonetheless take precedence over that of "free markets." The difference between the two is that the former implies public policy constraints on cyclical extremes, whereas the latter eschews public intervention of any sort. "Liberal" economic purity should not be the position of the United States with regard to world food markets.

7. *Global food interdependence is real and acceptable and its orderly management must be enhanced.* American policy should be guided by the recognition that this country is bound into complex relationships of interdependence in global food affairs that link not only our economic well-being but our political security to the behavior and aspirations of many other countries. Such interdependence is potentially benign, and international coordination and cooperation directed toward realizing this potential are urgent and legitimate. Contrariwise, unilateral actions, unless they are heedful of this interdependence, can be highly damaging to the global food system and should therefore be taken only with great care and after wide consultation.

The United States should not only be clear and emphatic in enunciating the principles of our international food policies, but its actions should also affirm its convictions. A pathway around possible world crises in food and agriculture in the years ahead requires elevating concern for the human beings who invariably become either beneficiaries of governments' wisdom or victims of their blunders. All of the principles that we encourage the United States government to support focus attention on satisfying people's basic needs for adequate nutrition. Though international relations have moved away from the era in which American preferences could be easily institutionalized as global norms, the United States is still preeminent in food affairs. The opportunity for leadership remains. What is called for now is patient yet persistent diplomacy to serve a renewed assertion of American moral authority.

Notes

1. Food Problems and the Policy Agenda

1. See, for instance, Keith Griffin, *Land Concentration and Rural Poverty* (New York: Holmes and Meier, 1976); Frances Moore Lappe and Joseph Collins, *Food First* (Boston: Houghton, Mifflin, 1977), and Cheryl Christensen, "World Hunger: A Structural Approach," in Raymond F. Hopkins and Donald J. Puchala, ed., *The Global Political Economy of Food* (Madison: University of Wisconsin Press, 1979), pp. 171-200.

2. See, for instance, Gary Seevers, "Food Markets and Their Regulation," in Hopkins and Puchala, *Global Political Economy of Food,* pp. 147-70.

3. These data were gathered during a project studying Politics, Communication, and Social Tension by Ronald D. Brunner of the University of Michigan. Sources are *The New York Times,* 1972-75, and the Gallup Poll, American Institute of Public Opinion, Princeton, N.J., 1972-76.

4. Based on comments by several officials who worked during part or all of this period on the White House economic policy staff, in the policy planning division of the State Department, or in the Department of Agriculture, e.g., Roger Porter, Carol Lancaster, Richard Bell, and Dale Hathaway.

5. See, for example, D. Gale Johnson, *World Agriculture in Disarray* (New York: Macmillan, 1973); D. Gale Johnson, *World Food Problems and Prospects* (Washington, D.C.: American Enterprise Institute for Public Policy Research, June 1975); Lester Brown with Erik Eckholm, *By Bread Alone* (New York: Praeger, 1974); Keith Griffin, *The Political Economy of Agrarian Change* (Cambridge: Harvard University Press, 1974).

6. USDA, *The World Food Situation and Prospects to 1985* (Washington, D.C.: United States Department of Agriculture, 1974); Lester Brown, "The World Food Prospect," *Science,* December 12, 1975, pp. 1053-59.

7. See U.S. Department of Agriculture, *Global Assessment Report* (Washington, D.C.: USDA, 1978), p. 46, table 2.

8. International Food Policy Research Institute, *Meeting Food Needs in the Developing World,* Research Report #1 (Washington, D.C.: IFPRI,

1976). Cf., also Raymond F. Hopkins and Donald J. Puchala, "Perspectives on the International Relations of Food," in Hopkins and Puchala, *Global Political Economy of Food,* pp. 283–98.

9. Michael W. Donnelly, "Japanese Agricultural Policy: The Political and Economic Dilemmas of Asia's New Giant," paper prepared for seminar on the Politics of Food, American Universities Field Staff, Rome, April 11–14, 1978; Fred H. Sanderson, *Japan's Food Prospects and Policies* (Washington, D.C.: Brookings Institution, 1978); Kenzo Hemmi, "Japan's Food Problems," paper presented at Conference on Food Policy and U.S.-Japanese Relations, Columbia University, March 1, 1977; See also, "Discussion Summary" from the Conference on Food Policy and U.S.-Japanese Relations, Columbia University, March 1, 1977.

10. Data are from FAO, *Food Outlook* (Rome: Food and Agriculture Organization, January 23, 1979), p. 20.

11. Lester Brown with Erik Eckholm, *By Bread Alone,* pp. 209–26 and Bruce F. Johnston and Peter Kilby, *Agriculture and Structural Transformation* (New York: Oxford University Press, 1975): Griffin, *Political Economy,* pp. 175–90.

12. Lawrence Hewes, *Rural Modernization: World Frontiers* (Ames: University of Iowa Press, 1974), pp. 34–82.

13. Griffin, *Political Economy,* pp. 210 ff; Griffin, *Land Concentration and Rural Poverty, passim;* Hewes, *Rural Modernization,* pp. 38–43; Susan George, *How the Other Half Dies* (Harmondsworth, Middlesex, England: Penguin Books, 1976), pp. 53–112; David Lehmann, ed., *Peasants, Landlords, and Governments: Agrarian Reform in the Third World* (New York: Holmes and Meier, 1974), pp. 13–24, 190–220 and *passim;* Solon L. Barraclough, "Interactions Between Agrarian Structure and Public Policies in Latin America," in Guy Hunter *et al.,* eds., *Policy and Practice in Rural Development* (Montclair, N.J.: Allanheld and Osmun, 1976), pp. 93–105.

14. Keith Griffin, *Underdevelopment in Spanish America* (Cambridge: M.I.T. Press, 1969).

15. Norman K. Nicholson and John D. Esseks, "The Politics of Food Scarcities in Developing Countries," in Hopkins and Puchala, *Global Political Economy of Food,* pp. 103–46. See also relevant articles in *Scientific American,* September 1976.

16. International Food Policy Research Institute, *Meeting Food Needs,* report no. 1.

17. James Austin, "Institutional Dimensions of the Malnutrition Prob-

lem," in Hopkins and Puchala, *Global Political Economy of Food,* pp. 237–64; Shlomo Reutlinger and Marcelo Selowsky, *Undernourishment and Poverty,* International Bank for Reconstruction and Development, Bank Staff Working Paper no. 202 (Washington, D.C.: IBRD, Apr. 1975); Lester Brown with Erik Eckholm, *By Bread Alone,* pp. 19–34, 179–208.

18. See Reutlinger and Selowsky, *Undernourishment and Poverty.*

19. See Lyle Schertz, "World Needs: Shall the Hungry Be with Us Always," in Peter G. Brown and Henry Shue, eds., *Food Policy: The Responsibility of the United States in Life and Death Choices* (New York: Free Press, 1977), pp. 13–35.

20. *Ibid.*

21. European countries, such as Britain and France in recent years, have inaugurated programs to assure adequate nutrition to the very poor; the U.S. food-stamp program began in 1963.

22. FAO, *Population, Food Supply and Agricultural Development* (Rome: Food and Agriculture Organization, 1975), page 28 as cited in the National Academy of Science, *World Food and Nutrition Study* (Washington, D.C.: NAS, 1977), p. 157.

23. See William Ascher, *Forecasting: An Appraisal for Policy-Makers and Planners* (Baltimore, Md.: Johns Hopkins University Press, 1978).

24. IFPRI, *Food Needs of Developing Countries: Projections of Production and Consumption to 1990.* Research Report no. 3. (Washington, D.C.: International Food Policy Research Institute, 1977), pp. 47–53.

25. Various estimates of losses from these factors have been attempted, ranging up to 40 per cent of total production. See, for example, the National Academy of Science, *World Food and Nutrition Study,* and *Agricultural Production Efficiency* (Washington, D.C.: National Academy of Sciences, 1974).

26. The survey by Eric Eckholm, *Losing Ground: Environmental Stress and World Food Prospects* (New York: Norton, 1976) is the best recent chronology of processes that are undermining soil fertility around the world.

27. On the importance of this factor see Keith Griffin, *The Political Economy of Agrarian Change,* and Michael Lipton, *Why Poor People Stay Poor* (Cambridge: Harvard University Press, 1976).

28. See FAO, *Assessment of the World Food Situation—Present and Future and the World Food Problem-Proposals for National and International Action* (Rome: Food and Agriculture Organization, Nov. 1974).

29. See J. De Hoogh, et al., *Food for a Growing World Population* (Amsterdam: Economic and Social Institute, February 1976), p. 4.

30. Almost all the recent literature on peasants emphasizes their "rational behavior" in response to circumstances. James Scott, in his book, *The Moral Economy of the Peasant* (New Haven: Yale University Press, 1977) emphasizes the often slim margin for "error" faced by peasants and their defensive orientations towards life that have evolved. Much greater emphasis on external constraints imposed from above, and hence the capacity of peasants to alter their behavior in response to positive incentives, as well as in response to their historical situation, are found in the works of Jeffrey Paige, *Agrarian Revolution* (New York: Free Press, 1975); Samuel Popkin, "Corporatism and Colonialism: The Political Economy of Rural Change in Vietnam," *Comparative Politics* (April 1976) 8:431–63; and Robert H. Bates, *Rural Responses to Industrialization* (New Haven: Yale University Press, 1976).

31. We want to thank Kenneth Lieberthal of Swarthmore College for calling this to our attention. In recent years, China's agriculture has grown at 2.6 percent, slightly above her rate of population growth. Although some experts are sanguine about China's future demands on world food markets, one economist forecasts a downturn in this growth in the 1980s to about 2 percent, making China a likely candidate to enter world grain markets on a continuing and rather substantial scale. See Robert F. Dornberger, "China's Economic Evolution and its Implication for the International System" (New York: Council on Foreign Relations 1980s Project, 1976), pp. 98–105. In the 1978/79 marketing year China again became a major grain importer continuing her irregular pattern of purchases.

32. This conclusion is fairly widespread among international agricultural experts, such as Clifton Wharton, who participated in the National Academy of Sciences, *World Food and Nutrition Study.*

33. See National Academy of Sciences, *Agriculture Production Efficiency.*

34. See Lipton, *Why Poor People Stay Poor.*

35. Louis Bean, a well-known statistician and forecast analyst for USDA, underlined this point in a seminar on food problems at Georgetown University, September 19, 1977. Bean argued that there is a complex but regular pattern to weather variations which, for example, allowed him to forecast accurately a depressed U.S. corn yield in 1974, which was the opposite of that forecast officially by USDA (Earl Butz) in January 1974.

36. See *Climate Change to the Year 2000* (Washington, D.C.,: National Defense University, USDA, NOAA, an Institute for the future, Feb. 1978), pages xvii–17. Also see the conclusions reported in "Global Food Interde-

pendence: Issues and Answers," INR (XRS-15, July 27, 1977. (Washington, D.C.: Department of State, 1977).

37. In this respect we differ with the mood of such analyses as those of Frances Moore Lappe and Joseph Collins, *Food First*, and Susan George, *How The Other Half Dies*.

2. The Commercial System:
The Political Economy of Food Trade

1. See Immanuel Wallerstein, *The Modern World-System: Capitalist Agriculture and the Origins of the European World Economy in the 16th Century* (New York: Academic Press, 1974), and Raymond F. Hopkins, Donald J. Puchala, and Ross B. Talbot, eds., *Food, Politics, and Agricultural Development* (Boulder, Colo: Westview, 1979).

2. We are indebted to James Kurth for reminding us of this result of food trade rivalry.

3. IFPRI, *Meeting Food Needs in the Developing World: The Location and Magnitude of the Task in the Next Decade*, Research Report no. 1. (Washington, D.C.: International Food Policy Research Institute, 1976), pp. 18–19; Central Intelligence Agency, Directorate of Intelligence, Office of Political Research, *Potential Implications of Trends in World Population, Food Production, and Climate*, OPR-401, August 1974, Appendix I, and IFPRI, *Food Needs of Developing Countries*. Research Report no. 3 (Washington, D.C.: IFPRI, December 1977), pp. 17–52.

4. Susan George, *How the Other Half Dies: The Real Reasons for World Hunger* (New York: Penguin, 1976); Cheryl Christensen, "World Hunger: A Structural Approach," *International Organization*, (Summer 1978), 32(3):745–74. Lyle P. Schertz, "World Food: Prices and the Poor," *Foreign Affairs*, (Apr. 1974), 52(3):511–37.

5. Helge Ole Bergesen, *When Interdependence Doesn't Work: A Study in World Food Politics* (Oslo: Norsk Untenrikspolitisk Institutt, 1977), p. 55.

6. *Ibid.*, p. 57.

7. Raymond F. Hopkins and Donald J. Puchala, "Perspectives on the International Relations of Food," in Hopkins and Puchala, eds., *The Global Political Economy of Food* (Madison: University of Wisconsin Press, 1979) pp. 3–40.

8. OECD, *Agricultural Policy in the United States* (Paris: Organization for Economic Cooperation and Development, 1974); OECD, *Agricultural Policy in Canada* (Paris: OECD, 1974).

9. Henry Nau, "The Diplomacy of World Food: Goals, Capabilities, Issues and Arenas," in Hopkins and Puchala, *Global Political Economy of Food,* pp. 211–12.

10. D. Gale Johnson, *World Agriculture in Disarray* (London and New York, Macmillan, 1973), pp. 28ff; Abdullah A. Saleh, "Disincentives to Agricultural Production in Developing Countries: A Policy Survey," *Foreign Agricultural Supplement* (Washington, D.C.: General Accounting Office, 1975).

11. D. Gale Johnson, *World Agriculture in Disarray:* FAO, *Agricultural Protection and Stabilization Policies: A Framework of Measurement in the Context of Agricultural Adjustment,* (Rome: Food and Agriculture Organization, 1975).

12. See, e.g., Bergesen, *Where Interdependence Doesn't Work,* pp. 70–75ff.

13. Michael W. Donnelly, "Japanese Agricultural Policy: The Political and Economic Dilemmas of Asia's New Giant," prepared for presentation at Seminar on "Politics of Food," Rome, American University Field Staff, April 11–14, 1978.

14. See Jack Shepherd, *The Politics of Starvation* (New York: Carnegie Endowment for International Peace, 1975). Governments fell in Ethiopia, Niger, and Bangladesh partly in response to 1974 food shortages. Riots broke out in Egypt in 1977 and Ghana in 1979 at even the threat of a food price rise.

15. UN World Food Conference, *Assessment of the World Food Situation: Present and Future,* Rome, 1974, E/CONF, 65/3,; Schertz, "World Food," p. 523–32. UN World Food Conference, *Report of the World Food Conference,* Rome, 1974, E/CONF. 65/20. p. 14–15.

16. Bergesen, *When Interdependence Doesn't Work,* p. 31; See also USDA, *The World Food Situation and Prospects to 1985,* Foreign Agricultural Economic Report #98. (Washington, D.C.: Dept. of Agriculture, 1974); FAO, *Report of the First Session of the Committee on World Food Security,* CL/70/10, April 1976.

17. IWC, *International Wheat Agreements: A Historical and Critical Background,* EX (74/75) 2/2, prepared for the second meeting of the Executive Committee (1974/75) (London: International Wheat Council, August 14, 1974).

18. *Ibid.,* p. 4.

19. In the United States, prices dropped to 50 percent of parity compared to 85 percent in 1952 and over 60 percent in 1928. See Wilfred Malenbaum, *The World Wheat Economy, 1885–1939* (Cambridge: Harvard University

Press, 1953), pp. 3–8. Malenbaum describes how wheat gradually replaced rye and other grains as the principal foodstuff in consumption and world trade over this period.

20. *International Wheat Agreements,* p. 14.

21. Simon Harris, *E.E.C. Trade Relations with the U.S.A. in Agricultural Products* (Ashford, Kent, England: Centre for European Agricultural Studies, 1977), pp. 16–18.

22. Robert Paarlberg, "Shifting and Sharing Adjustment Burdens: The Role of the Industrial Food Importing Nations," *International Organization* (Summer 1978), 32(3):655–78.

23. *Treaty Establishing the European Economic Community,* Rome, March 25, 1957 (London: H.M.S.O., 1973), pp. 18–22.

24. Stanley Andrews, *Agriculture and the Common Market* (Ames: Iowa State University Press, 1973), p. 19.

25. O ECD, *Agricultural Policy of the European Economic Community* (Paris: Organization for Economic Cooperation and Development, 1974), Annex.

26. Andrews, *Agriculture and the Common Market,* pp. 20–21.

27. Walter Hallstein, *Europe in the Making* (New York: Norton, 1972), pp. 178–92.

28. Lawrence Krause, *European Economic Integration and the United States* (Washington, D.C.: Brookings Institution, 1968), pp. 77ff.

29. Harris, *E.E.C. Trade Relations,* pp. 6–8.

30. *Ibid.,* p. 8.

31. William F. Averyt, *Agropolitics in the European Community: Interest Groups and the Common Agricultural Policy* (New York: Praeger, 1977): Glenda G. Rosenthal, *The Men Behind the Decisions* (Lexington, Mass.: Heath, 1975), pp. 79–100.

32. Agreements on dairy products were in fact contained in the Tokyo Round MTN Agreements signed in April 1979.

33. Harris, *E.E.C. Trade Relations,* pp. 23–25; Cf. also T. K. Warley, "Agriculture in International Economic Relations, "*American Journal of Agricultural Economics* (Dec. 1976), 58: 820–30.

34. Paarlberg, "Shifting and Sharing Adjustment Burdens," pp. 662–64.

35. See, for example, Raul Prebisch, *Toward a New Trade Policy for Development* (New York: United Nations Conference on Trade and Developments, 1964): A. S. Friedberg, *The United Nations Conference on Trade and Development of 1964* (Rotterdam: Rotterdam University Press, 1964)

36. Barbara Huddleston, *Commodity Trade Issues in International*

Negotiations, Occasional Paper No. 1 (Washington, D.C.: International Food Policy Research Institute, January 1977).

37. Michael Lipton, *Why the Poor Stay Poor* (Cambridge, Mass.: Harvard University Press, 1976).

38. In many cases we have been told that the U.S. "positive" attitude in the Carter Administration was peppered with considerable cynicism as well as technical and ideological opposition to many aspects of the commodity proposals of the United Nations Conference on Trade and Development.

39. Much LDC food processing to meet U.S. standards would require the import of American technology, managerial skill, and probably brand-name labeling, if not outright establishment of foreign subsidiaries.

40. For example, Susan George, *How the Other Half Dies;* See also Susan Demarco and Susan Sechler, *The Fields Have Turned Brown* (Washington, D.C.: The Agribusiness Accountability Project, 1975), pp. 67–93 and *passim.*

3. The Concessional System: From Dumping to Development

1. See Amalia Velliantis-Fidas and Eileen Mareau Manfredi, *P.L. 480 Concessional Sales* Foreign Agricultural Economic Report no. 142, (Washington D.C.: Economic Research Service, USDA, 1977), p. 1.

2. Ross M. Robertson, *History of the American Economy* (New York: Harcourt, Brace and World, 1964), p. 455.

3. Trudy Huskamp Peterson, "Hedge Against Hunger," (Washington, D.C.: mimeo., 1977) and personal communication, October 15, 1977, citing telegram #789, American Embassy in Bogota to the Department of State, June 17, 1954, available at the Eisenhower Library, Abilene, Kansas.

4. Velliantis-Fidas and Manfredi, *P.L. 480 Concessional Sales.*

5. Cited in James Bjorkman, "Public Law 480 and the Policies of Self-Help and Short-Tether: Indo-American Relations, 1965–68," *Report of the Commission on the Organization of the Government for the Conduct of Foreign Policy,* Appendix vol. 7 (Washington, D.C.: GPO, 1976), p. 203.

6. See Mitchel B. Wallerstein, "The Politics of International Food Aid: U.S. Policy Objectives in an Evolving Multilateral Context" (Ph.D. dissertation, MIT, 1978).

7. See Paul J. Isenman and Hans W. Singer, "Food Aid: Disincentive Effects and their Policy Considerations," *Economic Development and Cultural Change* (January 1977), 25:205–238.

8. A strong argument is made that nearly all aid recipients in this period, since they all had large and expensive commercial imports, would have, if necessary, also imported the food sent as aid on commercial terms. If true, then food aid has no inflationary effect, it only reduced American export earnings.

9. See the report by Joseph F. Stepanek, "Food for Development: A Food Aid Policy" (Washington, D.C.: Agency for International Development Memorandum, March 16, 1978, mimeo.).

10. See Emma Rothchild, "Is It Time to End Food for Peace," *New York Times Magazine,* March 13, 1977, pp. 15, 43–48. In particular, Rothchild argued that food aid was often subordinated to commercial interests, such as promoting sales of rice from producing states, and had deleterious effects on farm income and agricultural policy in recipient countries. Her judgement, shared by many economists, is that equivalent money supplied to recipient countries in the form of cash would better serve their economic development.

11. Interview with Mead, January 1975.

12. This view is widely held among development economists, promoted by United Nations and the United Nations Conference on Trade and Development (UNCTAD) and has seldom been disputed as a general point.

13. See John D. Montgomery, *Foreign Aid in International Politics* (Englewood Cliffs, N.J.: Prentice-Hall, 1967); Robert Rothstein, *The Weak in the World of the Strong* (New York: Columbia University Press, 1977); David Wall, *The Charity of Nations* (New York: Basic Books, 1973). Charles Frank and Mary Baird, "Foreign Aid: Its Speckled Past and Future Prospects," in C. Fred Bergsten and Larry B. Krause, eds., *World Politics and International Economics* (Washington, D.C.: Brookings Institution, 1975), and Lester B. Pearson et al., *Partners in Development* (New York: Praeger, 1969).

14. This could occur when a country had a strong urban bias which it refused to alter and which food aid would reinforce. See Michael Lipton, *Why Poor People Stay Poor* (Cambridge: Harvard University Press, 1976).

15. See Uma K. Srivastava, et al., *Food Aid and International Economic Growth* (Ames: Iowa State University Press, 1975); *Food Aid Policies and Programs: A Study of Surveys of Food Aid* (Rome: World Food Program, 1978), a study by Professor Hans W. Singer; and interim report: "An Assessment of Development Assistant Strategies" (Washington, D.C.: Brookings Institution, October 1977), a study for the Department of State by Lester E. Gordon, pp. 33–36.

16. Paul J. Isenman and Hans W. Singer, "Food Aid: Disincentive Effects."

17. Lance Taylor, "The Misconstrued Crisis," *World Development* (December 1975), 3(11,12):827–37.

18. For the importance of this in affecting peasant farmers, see David K. Leonard, *Reaching the Peasant Farmer: Organization Theory and Practice in Kenya* (Chicago: University of Chicago Press, 1977).

19. See Peterson, "Hedge Against Hunger."

20. See Wallerstein, "Politics of International Food Aid."

21. In earlier years, a Title III and Title IV existed in the PL480 legislation that allowed for government-to-government sales and for barter of food for other raw materials which the United States sought to stockpile after the Korean War. These titles have been rescinded and the new Title III ("Food for Development") is distinctly different from these earlier titles.

22. See Donald McHenry and Kai Bird, "Food Bungle in Bangladesh," *Foreign Policy* (Summer 1977), 27:72–88.

23. See Lloyd I. and Susan Hoever Rudolph, "The Coordination of Complexity in South Asia," in *Report of the Commission on the Organization of the Government for the Conduct of Foreign Policy,* appendix vol. 7 (Washington, D.C.: GPO , 1976), p. 125.

24. Among the many studies that make this point, see Morton Halperin, *Bureaucratic Politics and Foreign Policy* (Washington, D.C.: Brookings Institution, 1974); Hugh Heclo, *A Government of Strangers* (Washington, D.C.: Brookings Institution, 1977); and various studies for the Commission on the Organization of the Government: See, for example, *Report.* Political leadership can be sabotaged if senior bureaucrats are ideologically opposed to a course of action or see it conflicting with their own interest. Helco notes

that for the mixed collection of senior civil servants who interact with political executives, power is not typically derived from refusing to do what their superiors want. Absolutely passive compliance to political superiors—"Yes, boss" approach— can be the easiest means to obstructing political leadership if bureaucrats are so inclined.

By not protecting their political superiors when they have ideas that will turn out badly or wreak havoc due to technical problems, a program or leader can be undermined as effectively as by delay or obfuscation.

4. Organizing the Executive Branch for Foreign Food Policy

1. The Department of State, the Agency for International Development, and the Treasury all had a role in foreign policy of course, indeed increasing ones after the mid-1960s.

2. See Edward Schuh, "The New Macroeconomics of Agriculture," *American Journal of Agricultural Economics* (December 1976), 58:803–7; and Schuh, "World Food Production and International Trade," (Washington, D.C.: Paper prepared for Food and Agricultural Policy Conference at the American Enterprise Institute, March 10–11, 1977).

3. For example, the senior review group created by OMB in 1973 was chaired by Philip Dusault, director of the Economics section of the International Affairs Division, whose training includes a B.A. from Harvard in history and literature and a stint in the Peace Corps before joining OMB in 1967; the three heads of State's Office of Food Policy in 1974–78 were all career generalists with some economic specialization but no advanced degrees, while over half the top officials in Agriculture's Internal Affairs Division have had Ph.D.s in Agricultural Economics.

4. Worthington was a former official in both the Agriculture and State Departments and had just completed the "Flanigan" report for the Nixon administration, the major background analysis of possible benefits from lower trade barriers written as a prelude to negotiations on agricultural tariffs and non-tariff barriers in the trade talks of the MTN. *Agricultural Trade and the Proposed Round of Multilateral Negotiations,* Council on International Economic Policy (Washington, D.C.: U.S. Government Printing Office, 1973).

5. President Carter's reorganization project for food and nutrition policy finds safety, nutrition, and foreign policy concerns dispersed among 22 agencies other than the Department of Agriculture. General Accounting Office, *Issues Surrounding the Management of Agricultural Exports,* (Washington, D.C.: GAO, May 2, 1977), 1:6.

6. Presidential Reorganization Project, Office of Management and Budget, "Food and Nutrition Policy: Issue Summary" (Washington, D.C.: draft of 7/27/1977, 1. Mimeo.

7. For a series of critiques and rebuttals, see *Who's Making Foreign Agricultural Policy?* Hearings before the Subcommittee on Foreign Agricultural Policy of the Committee on Agriculture and Forestry, U.S. Senate, January 22–23, 1976 (Washington, D.C.: GPO, 1976).

8. See Roger Morris, *Disaster in the Desert* (Washington, D.C.: Carnegie Foundation, 1975).

9. Such a view was advocated by Roger B. Porter at the Conference on Global Food Interdependence, April 7–9, 1977, in his paper "On Organizing U.S. Food and Agricultural Policymaking."

10. Interview with subcabinet USDA official, April, 1977.

11. See Raymond F. Hopkins, "Global Management Networks: The

Internationalization of Domestic Bureaucracies," *International Social Science Journal,* (January 1978), 30(1):31–46.

12. See Schuh, "World Food Production," p. 15.

13. For a fuller account of these episodes, see I. M. Destler, "U.S. Food Policy 1972–1976," in Hopkins and Puchala, *Global Political Economy of Food,* pp. 41–78.

14. Joseph Gavin, "The Bureaucratic Politics of Agricultural Export Policy: Grain Sales to the Soviet Union, 1974," paper at the International Studies Association (Washington, D.C.: February 22–25, 1978), p. 38.

15. See Harold Seidman, *Politics, Position and Power* (New York: Oxford University Press, 1975).

16. See Michael C. Jensen, "Industry Role Scored in Trade Talks," *New York Times* (June 14, 1978) pp. D1, D19. Hathaway rebutted attacks by arguing that such nongovernmental associates "have technical knowledge of how wheat is sold and traded." And "they gave us some parameters of what the growers consider acceptable."

17. See Hopkins, "Global Management Networks."

5. American Multilateral Food Diplomacy: The United States Role in International Organizations

1. U.S. Senate, Select Committee on Nutrition and Human Needs, *The United States, FAO, and World Food Politics: U.S. Relations with An International Food Organization* (Washington, D.C.: GPO, June 1976), pp. 11–13. Hereafter this Senate document will be cited as the "Percy Report."

2. Martin Kriesberg, *International Organizations and Agricultural Development* Foreign Agricultural Economic Report No. 133, (Washington, D.C.: U.S. Dept. of Agriculture, Economic Research Service, May 1977) pp. 31–33.

3. *Ibid.,* p. 36.

4. *Ibid.,* p. 32.

5. World Food Conference, *Report of the World Food Conference,* (Rome: 1974), E/Conf. 65/20 p. 18; See also, Robin Sharp, "The World Food Council: More Than a Garnish?" *Food Policy* (Nov. 1975), 1(1):84–86; Thomas G. Weiss and Robert S. Jordan, *The World Food Conference and Global Problem Solving* (New York: Praeger, 1976), p. 68.

6. *Report of the World Food Council on its Fourth Session,* June 12–15, 1978, General Assembly Official Records, 33d Session, Supplement #19, A/33/19.

7. World Food Conference, *Report of the World Food Conference,* p. 13.

8. Consultative Group on International Agricultural Research, *CGIAR* (New York: CGIAR, 1976), p. 4ff.

9. B. Gosovic, *UNCTAD, Conflict and Compromise: The Third World's Quest for an Equitable World Order Through the United Nations* (Leiden: Sijthoff, 1975), pp. 93–114 and *passim.*; J. C. Nagle, *Agricultural Trade Policies* (Lexington, Mass.: Heath, 1976), pp. 70–79.

10. *Percy Report,* pp. 25–28.

11. Several United States delegates to FAO meetings interviewed in the course of our research, especially individuals who attended during earlier periods, expressed dismay and discomfort at the aggressive and "unsound" views put forward by many of the newer nations' representatives.

12. *U.S. Participation in the Food and Agriculture Organization of the United Nations,* Hearings Before the Select Committee on Nutrition and Human Needs of the United States Senate, 94th Cong. 2d Sess., March 4–5, 1976, pp. 93–94.

13. *Ibid.,* p. 94.

14. *Ibid.,* p. 105.

15. *Ibid.,* pp. 118–19.

16. FAO, *Proposal by the Director-General on International Action to Assure Basic Food Stocks,* FAO Council, 60th Session, CL60/11 (Rome: Food and Agriculture Organization May 1973); *World Food Security, Proposal of the Director-General,* FAO Conference, 17th Session, C73/17 (Rome: Aug. 1973).

17. OECD, *Agricultural Policy in the United States* (Paris: Organization for Economic Cooperation and Development, 1974), p. 103 and *passim;* OECD, *Agricultural Policy in Canada* (Paris: OECD, 1974), *passim.*

18. I. M. Destler, "U.S. Food Policy 1972–1976: Reconciling Domestic and International Objectives," *International Organization* (Summer 1978), 32(3):617–44.

19. U.S. Congress, Office of Technology Assessment, *Food Information Systems* (Washington, D.C.: GPO, June 1975), pp. 61–70; See also, *Food Information Systems,* Hearings Before the Technology Assessment Board of the Office of Technology Assessment, 94th Cong. 1st and 2d Sessions, September 24, 25 and December 10, 1975, February 4, 1976 (Washington, D.C.: U.S. GPO, 1976), pp. 70–81 and *passim*; David A. Kay, "The Behavior of International Organizations in the World Food Arena," in Giulio Pontecorvo, ed., *The Management of Food Policy* (New York: Arno Press, 1976), pp. 123–25.

20. Joseph M. Jones, *The United Nations at Work: Developing Land, Forests, Oceans and People* (Oxford, England: Pergamon Press, 1965), p. 118ff.

21. Consultative Group, *GGIAR*, pp. 11–67.

22. Lester Brown, *Seeds of Change* (New York: Overseas Development Council, 1970).

23. Kriesberg, *International Organizations, passim.*; Jones, *United Nations at Work, passim.*; USDA, *Multilateral Assistance for Agricultural Development* (Washington, D.C.: U.S. Department of Agriculture/ERS, Oct. 1973).

24. *Percy Report,* pp. 20–25.

25. Kriesberg, *International Organizations,* p. 68; Montague Yudelman, "The World Bank and Agricultural Development," in Pontecorvo, ed., *Management of Food Policy,* pp. 17–36; Susan George, *How the Other Half Dies* (Harmondsworth, Middlesex, England: Penguin Books, 1976), pp. 235–64.

26. Inis Claude, *The Changing United Nations* (New York: Random House, 1967), pp. 74–104.

27. Robert L. Bard, *Food Aid and International Agricultural Trade* (Lexington, Mass.: Heath, 1972), pp. 111–30.

28. *Percy Report,* pp. 3–4.

29. Helge Ole Bergesen, *When Interdependence Doesn't Work: A Study in World Food Politics* (Oslo: Norsk Utenrikspolitisk Institutt, 1977), pp. 89–93ff.

30. See chapter 2 above; Simon Harris, *E.E.C. Trade Negotiations with the U.S.A. in Agricultural Products* (Ashford, Kent, England: Centre for European Agricultural Studies, 1977), pp. 9–14.

31. See chapter 2 above; Bergesen, *When Interdependence Doesn't Work,* pp. 158–61.

32. *U.S. Participation,* Hearings, pp. 78–86.

33. *Ibid.,* pp. 1, 16, 127ff.; *Percy Report,* pp. 2–3.

34. *U.S. Participation,* Hearings, pp. 78–86 and 107.

6. The Framework for Future United States Policy: Assessing Alternative Risks

1. For a discussion of the importance of such developmental constructs in policy analysis, see Harold Lasswell, *The Future of Political Science* (New York: Atheneum, 1963).

2. This scenario is most in line with that of the primary trend suggested by the study on climate change and by other projections. See, Research

Directorate of the National Defense University, *Climate Change in the Year 2000* (Washington: National Defense Univ., 1978).

3. We raised this point explicitly with over forty experts on world food affairs (representing a variety of expertise, including commercial trade, economic analysis, bureaucratic politics, agricultural science, nutrition, and political and economic history). They asserted that another shortage period nearly as, or somewhat more severe than, that of the early 1970s was generally to be expected without the adoption of policies mandating substantial reserves. Some, such as Sterling Wortman, foresaw even more serious prospects without imaginative new efforts to address food problems.

4. See Lester Brown, *By Bread Alone* (New York: Praeger, 1974); Eckholm, *Losing Ground* and Georg Borgstrom, *The Food and People Dilemma* (North Scituate, Mass.: Duxbury Press, 1973).

5. Unfortunately, policymakers seldom fully appreciate the importance of this quality of acceptance of governmental legitimacy because of its diffuse and less volatile character. See, for example, Raymod F. Hopkins, "Establishing Authority: A View from the Top," *World Politics* (Jan. 1972), 24:271–72; and Ronald Rogowski, *National Legitimacy* (Princeton, N.J.: Princeton University Press, 1974).

6. See, for example, the Report by the Central Intelligence Agency (August, 1974) OPR-401, "Potential Implications of Trends in World Population, Food Production, and Climate" and Reid A. Bryceson and Thomas S. Murry, *Climates of Hunger* (Madison: University of Wisconsin Press, 1977). It might also be argued that projections by the International Food Policy Research Institute (IFPRI) also lend themselves to such interpretation, especially if poor food importing countries turn for a year or two during shortages to the commercial system.

7. On such effects in Nigeria, see Gerald Helleiner, *Peasant Agriculture, Government, and Economic Growth in Nigeria* (Homewood, Ill.: Irwin, 1966); and more generally Bates, *Rural Responses to Industrialization,* and Lipton, *Why the Poor Stay Poor.*

8. The 1972–73 shortfall was less than 2 percent—compared to the 1971–72 crop—yet it led to a tripling and quadrupling in the price of key commodities. Among individual producers, the Soviet Union is especially vulnerable. Because only 1 percent of the Soviet Union has an average annual rainfall of 28 inches or more, compared to 69 percent of the arable land of the United States, and because two-thirds of Soviet agriculture lies north of the Fortieth parallel, whereas almost all of the United States is below this line, weather variations have had substantially larger effects on supply instability

in the Soviet Union because of its small margin around favorable crop conditions. Surprisingly, Soviet efforts at grain storage are far behind those of the United States. Both problems of management and technical problems such as adequate drying of grain have until very recently deterred the Soviets from undertaking large stockpiling activities.

9. See Wayne D. Rasmussen, ed., *A History of American Agriculture* (Washington, D.C.: USDA, 1972 Yearbook of Agriculture) for a description of surplus stock programs.

10. See, for example, Max Milner et al., eds., *Protein Resources and Technology* (Westport, Conn.: AVI Publishing, 1978), esp. the article by Raymond Hopkins and Anthony Pryor, "The Politics of New Protein," pp. 97–110.

11. Fairly optimistic prospects are suggested by Roger Revell and Peter Jennings in articles in the special issue of *Scientific American*, "Food and Agriculture," (Sept. 1976), 235:164–195. The decline of growth in American agriculture and a forecast of rising future costs as increasing marginal gains are derived from less fertile land or additional chemical inputs are described in James G. Horsfall and Charles R. Frink, "Perspective on Agriculture's Future Rising Cost-Raising Doubts," (New Haven: Connecticut Agricultural Experiment Station, 1975). Manuscript.

12. The problem of burden sharing in obtaining the collective goods of food security and stability, particularly should the United States and Canada have substantial surpluses, will be difficult. Sometimes individuals and countries will not provide voluntary contributions, thereby forgoing a collective good each would willingly pay a proportionate share to secure, because there is a lack of organization to enforce cost sharing. On this point see Mancur Olson, Jr., *The Logic of Collective Action* (Cambridge: Harvard University Press, 1965).

13. See Richard N. Cooper, "Economic Interdependence and Foreign Policy in the 70s," *World Politics* (Jan. 1972). 24(2):pp. 159–81.

14. See *Impact of Climatic Fluctuation on Major North American Food Crops* (Dayton, Ohio: Charles F. Kettering Foundation, Institute of Ecology, 1976), p. 14.

15. The concept of "free-rider" is outlined in Olson, *Logic of Collective Action*. The Soviet Union's disruptive grain purchases in 1972, for example, forced the burden of adjustment to tight world supplies onto the United States and many poor developing countries. The Soviets acted as a "free-rider" on the global trading system, and the bilateral Soviet-American grain agreement of 1975, plus tightened government monitoring of (and inter-

vention in) grain trading, were steps by the United States to limit such free-riding.

7. Global Food Interdependence and the Challenge to American Policy

1. See especially suggestions for research put forward in chapter 3.

2. W. A. Douglas Jackson, ed., *Agrarian Policies and Problems in Communist and Non-Communist Countries* (Seattle: University of Washington Press, 1971); Elizabeth and Graham Johnson, *Walking on Two Legs: Rural Development in South China* (Ottawa: International Development Research Center, 1976).

3. Susan George, *How the Other Half Dies* (Hammondsworth, Middlesex, England: Penguin, 1976).

Index

International Labor Organization, 134
International Monetary Fund, exerts
pressure on Egypt, 90
International-research facility, 58
International Wheat Agreement (IWA),
1933, 52; 1949, 53; 1952, 1956, 53;
1962, 54; 1967, 54; market prices
1949–53, 55; 77
International Wheat Convention (IWC),
142, 148
International Wheat Council, 53, 56,
134
Iran, 20, 79
Isenman, Paul, 99
Israel, 89, 90, 91, 134
Issues:
——in food trade, 2, 157, 170; transfer,
11; liberalization, 50, 60; market
stability, 176–78
——in food aid, 2, 30, 49; transfer, 11;
historically, 72–77; goals, 77; policy,
78–106; multilateral vs. bilateral,
106–8; in international organizations,
146; as weapon, 151–53; uses in
development, 184, 186; *see also* Food
power
——in food policy-making, xiii, xv,
28–31, 111–17, 118–26, European
Community, 64; European
Community-U.S., 67;
considerations, 123; consistency, 147;
options, 150–59; U.S., 184–88
——in international organization,
128–29; concessional terms, 51;
historically, 52–56; U.S. role in,
127–30; 140–45, 174–75;
International Food Organizations,
130–34; as solution, 181–82

Jaenke, Edward A., 115, 116
Jamaica, 151; food aid to, 87
Japan, 11, 20, 25, 41, 48, 49, 59, 79, 119,
120, 121, 152, 153, 154, 178; exports,
13–14; malt market, 66

Johnson, Lyndon, 91, 104, 105
Jones, Brennon, 125

Kennedy administration, 104
Kennedy Round, 65
Kerala, 171
Kissinger, Henry, xv, 88, 89, 151
Korean War, 57, 73

Land: underemployment, 14, 25–27;
resource input for food production,
24–25; fertility, 24–25; barriers to use,
25–26
Land reform, 102
Latin America, 14
Legitimacy, 144–145
Less Developed Countries (LDC); *see*
Third World
Lewis, Samuel W., 136

McGovern, George, 104
Malnutrition, 103, 151, 158–59; 163,
165, 169; chronic, 3, 15–17, 154;
solutions to, 16
Malt, markets in Japan, 66
Mansholt Plan, 61, 66
Market: international instability, 9, 58;
competition for advantage, 34;
sharing, 53; EC concerns, 64; CAP
insulation from world, 66; "stealing,"
80; stability, 176–78; stability should
be enhanced, 187
Marshall Plan, 73
Mead, Arthur, 93
Mexico, 79, 80
MIT-Harvard Nutrition Policy
Program, 21–22
Montgomery, John, 97
Multilateral Trade Negotiations (MTN),
1978, 125, 142, 178

National Academy of Sciences, 114, 158
National Science Foundation, 114
National Security Council (NSC), 112,
115, 119

weeks